Sue Simkins works as a recipe developer and writes recipe columns for several monthly magazines including *Best of British*, *Country Smallholding* and the *Countryman*. Her recipes cover the whole range of wholesome home cooking with plenty of baking. They are the kind of recipes that novice and experienced cooks will all enjoy: simple and delicious with helpful tips and explanations. Sue lives in Dorset with her family.

522 761 57 5

Also by Sue Simkins

Cooking with Mrs Simkins

Cakes from the Tooth Fairy

Fresh Bread and Bakes from your Bread Machine

How to Make the Most of Your Food Processor

Afternoon Tea

Delicious cakes, pastries, biscuits and savouries
for every day and special occasions

SUE SIMKINS

RIGHT
WAY

Constable & Robinson Ltd
55–56 Russell Square
London WC1B 4HP
www.constablerobinson.com

First published in the UK by Spring Hill,
an imprint of How to Books, 2010

This edition published by Right Way,
an imprint of Constable & Robinson Ltd, 2014

Copyright © Sue Simkins 2010, 2014

The right of Sue Simkins to be identified as the author of this work has
been asserted by her in accordance with the Copyright, Designs & Patents
Act 1988.

All rights reserved. This book is sold subject to the condition that it shall
not, by way of trade or otherwise, be lent, re-sold, hired out or otherwise
circulated in any form of binding or cover other than that in which it is
published and without a similar condition including this condition being
imposed on the subsequent purchaser.

A copy of the British Library Cataloguing in Publication Data
is available from the British Library

ISBN: 978-0-71602-370-8 (paperback)
ISBN: 978-0-71602-376-0 (ebook)

1 3 5 7 9 10 8 6 4 2

Printed and bound in the EU

Contents

Acknowledgements

I would like to thank my family and friends and everyone who helped with the making of this book.

Special thanks to Moira Blake of Dorset Pastry, Deidre Hills and all the members of the Marnhull Mothers' Union, Adrian Curtis (Family Butcher), Clive Mellum of Shipton Mills, and to Claire Tuck, Daniel Parr and everyone at Clipper Teas who kindly supplied tea notes an pages 172–179.

As ever, thank you to Fanny Charles and everyone at the Blackmore Vale Magazine.

And finally, a huge thank you to everyone at Constable & Robinson.

Thank you all very much indeed.

Introduction

Helpful Equipment

Here are the most useful sizes of baking tins, most of which are used in this book. Heavier, better quality baking tins conduct heat more efficiently than anything thin and flimsy. They also have a longer life.

Large baking tray

A baking tray that just fits comfortably inside your oven can be used for all kinds of bread and biscuits and scones.

Standard 20cm (8in) square brownie tin

This is a really useful size and shape for brownies and small tray bakes.

12-cup muffin tin

As well as muffins this is perfect for buns, rolls, fairy cakes and deep-filled tarts.

12-cup mini-muffin tin

A couple of these are useful for tiny cakes and tarts.

12-cup tart tins

It's useful to have a couple of these for tarts, mince pies and small quiches.

Loose-bottomed cake, sandwich and flan tins

It's handy to have the following sizes:
18cm (7in) cake tin; pair of 18cm (7in) sandwich tins; 20cm (8in) cake tin; 20cm (8in) flan tin; 23cm (9in) cake tin – particularly if you make your own Christmas cake.

Loose-bottomed 10cm (4in) tartlet tins

Often sold in packs of six, these are perfect for elegant individual fruit tarts and also for individual quiches and savoury flans.

Mini loaf tins

Often sold in packs of four, these are brilliant for sweet, dinky, little loaves of bread and bar cakes. It's useful to have 12, but they're not cheap so it's worth knowing they hold the same amount of mix as the cup of a 12-cup muffin tin – enabling you to make a mixed batch.

Look after them carefully to keep them in good condition: instead of scrubbing them in hot soapy water or throwing them in the dishwasher, it's usually possible to clean them perfectly well by wiping with kitchen paper.

Ceramic baking beans

Treat yourself to some proper ceramic baking beans: two tubs would be ideal. Ceramic baking beans conduct the heat more efficiently than dried peas or beans when baking pastry flan cases blind. They help to conduct heat to the inside of the pastry case as well as weighing it down and supporting the sides.

Oven Temperature Conversions

Mark 1	275°F	140°C
Mark 2	300°F	160°C
Mark 3	332°F	170°C
Mark 4	350°F	180°C
Mark 5	375°F	200°C
Mark 6	400°F	220°C
Mark 7	425°F	230°C
Mark 8	450°F	230°C

Please be aware that individual oven performance varies greatly.

Measurements

Both metric and imperial measurements are given for the recipes. Follow one set of measurements, not a mixture of both, as they are not interchangeable.

1. All Kinds of Tea Time Occasions

Afternoon Tea had very aristocratic beginnings. Although tea drinking started in Britain in the 17th century, sitting around, drinking tea with cakes and delicate little savouries came later.

By the 19th century, among the upper classes, lunch was served at midday and, for various reasons, dinner had become a very late meal: 8 o'clock at the earliest, with nothing in between. Ladies were obliged to order a pot of tea during the afternoon along with a little something to keep them going. Eventually, friends and family were invited and the concept of Afternoon Tea began. And so it became a convivial opportunity for the ladies of the house and their friends to relax together and chat, as well as to stop their blood sugar levels from plummeting!

A kettle would be boiled on a small spirit stove near the tea table and the lady of the house would make the tea in a silver or bone china teapot. The food would be very delicate and refined: thinly cut bread and butter, cucumber sandwiches made with the slenderest slivers of peeled cucumber, dainty cakes on a pretty cake stand, and possibly something toasted in a covered silver dish served during the cold days of winter.

High Tea, on the other hand, came about out of necessity, once the Industrial Revolution had turned the majority of working people away from their home-based jobs and into the factories and mills. It was a substantial meal for the whole family at the end of a hard working day, as hearty as funds would permit, and brought to the table with the minimum of effort and accompanied by cups of strong tea.

Most of the family members would very likely have been working all day and would arrive home tired and hungry with little energy or inclination, or even a hot stove or fire, to cook.

During the 19th century tea had come down in price and was first drunk by the working classes as a precious treat, but as prices fell even more it turned into a household staple and was drunk at every mealtime, and often in between as well.

Afternoon Tea is so called because it is based around cups of tea taken in the afternoon, but why is High Tea called *High* Tea? It may very well be because whereas Afternoon Tea was taken whilst sitting in low easy chairs and sofas, with everything set out on small tables, High Tea was eaten whilst sitting 'up' at a full size table on a hard chair or bench.

Maybe, it was because the plates were piled high as working people tucked into their main meal of the day!

Afternoon Tea is usually served earlier in the afternoon, towards 4 o'clock. It is based around 'finger food' although special little cake forks can be used for creamier cakes and pastries. You may also have small 'tea knives' if toast and the spreading of sweet or savoury toppings is involved.

High Tea is served much later, from 5 o'clock, but usually around 6 o'clock. It is partly based around food eaten with a knife and fork: in fact High Tea is sometimes referred to as a 'Knife and Fork Tea' or a 'Meat Tea'. Typical dishes served for High Tea, depending upon the household budget, could be: cold meats, particularly ham, and meat pies such as pork pie or pasties, often served with pickles or relishes; fish, maybe fried fish or kippers; or dishes with cheese or eggs; and plenty of bread in the form of thickly sliced bread and butter, rolls or toast or toasted crumpets, muffins and fruit breads. There might be a cake component to round off the meal. Later, tinned fruit and tinned fish became popular as well.

For some of us, the last meal of the day is still thought of as 'tea'. Others may call it dinner, supper or the evening meal.

MIL or MIF? Milk in first? Milk in last?

This is a complete minefield. Many people feel that the tea should be poured first with milk added afterwards, and this is *the only* civilised way to serve tea. Some of us feel that the milk should be poured into the cup first and the tea poured on top, as this way the milk and the tea 'blend' better and you can tell instantly 'if the colour is right'. There is also talk of the hot tea slightly 'scalding' the milk when you do it this way; some people say this improves the taste, others say it doesn't.

There is also the possibility of the hot tea cracking the (usually surprisingly robust) bone china cups, which could become very cold in the unheated houses of the 19th century and therefore vulnerable to the action of the hot tea upon them. In some cases this view could lead to milk in first to prevent the cup from cracking. In others, possibly, it could be milk in last, to show that a few cracked cups here and there were of little consequence as you could buy new ones whenever you felt like it!

Which milk?
If you are taking milk in your tea, now that we have so many types to choose from, which milk *should* you choose? Many of us feel that full cream or whole milk is too creamy, skimmed milk is too watery and semi-skimmed milk is just right.

Who's Mother?
Generally, the woman of the house is in charge of the teapot and pours everyone's tea for them. If there is no woman of the house or tea is taken out, in a tea shop or hotel perhaps, somebody will be chosen to pour the tea and be 'Mother'. That person will then be in sole charge of the teapot throughout the meal and nobody else should try to pour from it. 'Mother' should be on the alert to the possibility of the others in the party wanting their cups refilled and should be the one to add more hot water to the teapot as necessary.

Picnic Tea
A picnic is really any kind of combination of food and drink enjoyed outside. It can be a grand affair with enormous wicker hampers and proper china and glassware, but it is more usually fairly informal and simple. It's more likely to be sandwiches and cake with flasks of tea and bottles of soft drinks eaten on a rug spread on the ground.

The great British picnic conjures up childhood memories of sandy sandwiches on the beach sheltered by a stripy windbreak – not so much to protect you and your food from the wind but from all the beach balls whizzing about.

These days, you can arm yourself for a picnic with every type of equipment you could possibly want: cool boxes and freezer blocks, a staggering array of bright and cheerful unbreakable cups and plates, wide-necked flasks, folding chairs that aren't too heavy and are actually comfy, little pop-up tents and sun shades, waterproof rugs and, instead of the old soapy flannel in a plastic bag, you can take wet wipes and hand gels.

TV Tea

Although slobbing out in front of the TV for every meal is definitely not to be encouraged, there is something very cosy and relaxing about a companionable family tea in front of the TV. The key is that you watch a programme or film that you all enjoy, the tea things spread out on the coffee table within easy reach.

If it's winter, you might have a fire to sit round as well. When it's chilly and dark outside and you are all tucked up inside with the curtains drawn, toast and toasted crumpets are a particularly welcome treat. There is nothing to stop you bringing the toaster in on a tray rather then dashing backwards and forwards to the kitchen.

You might like to try some savoury spreads and potted meats: the **Original Cheddar Spread** is fabulous on crumpets, the **Potted Meats** and **Fish Pastes**, great on hot buttered toast.

Cricket Tea

The gentle thwack of leather on willow, perfect blue summer skies, stripy deck chairs, players in cricket whites alternately standing around expectantly or breaking into a sudden run, the pavilion in the distance with the promise of tea . . .

A typical cricket tea is intended to be eaten milling around with a plate in one hand and might consist of: plates of sandwiches cut into triangles and resting on their backs – maybe garnished with tomatoes cut into quarters, possibly some miniature Melton Mowbray pork pies or some really good sausage rolls, scones split in half with jam and a dollop of cream already on them, chocolate cake, lemon cake and fruit cake – all cut into slices, and some mixed pastries such as jam and lemon curd tarts.

If you are providing ham sandwiches and pork pies, don't forget to put some mustard on the table.

Cream Tea

The cream tea is such an English tradition: lovely light scones, thick cream (preferably clotted) and strawberry jam, all served with a generous pot of tea.

The way a cream tea is served is practically as important as the food itself. It should be very traditional, either at a refined tea table with a silver or bone china tea pot and delicate cups and saucers, or cottagey and countrified with pretty, mismatched china and a jug of garden flowers on the table, all jostling for space with the little glass dishes of cream and jam. And if the weather is nice, what could be more perfect on a summer's day than a cream tea served outside in a (wasp-free) country garden?

✓ A note on jam

The quality of the jam is just as important as the scones and cream. Many a cream tea has been a bit of a let-down when a jellified blob of something, corresponding to no known fruit, is found lurking in the jam dish.

Strawberry jam, preferably homemade, is the most traditional choice. A few sliced strawberries on the side, freshly picked and still warm from the sun, are always appreciated.

Strawberry Tea

There's nothing like a strawberry tea in the garden on a balmy day in early summer. It's like a kind of super cream tea with added strawberries. You can serve plenty of **Scones**, with **Strawberry Jam** and cream with bowls of strawberries as well.

Blackberry Tea

Sometimes, you don't quite want to let go of the summer: even though the school holidays are just about over and the strawberries are long gone, you might fancy a bit of a tea party in the garden before autumn sets in. What you can do is have a blackberry tea.

If you are near a blackberry patch you can start off the proceedings by going blackberrying and then come back to a tea with a bit of a blackberry and early autumn theme.

Instead of strawberry jam with your scones, you could have blackberry jelly or crab apple jelly and make a sponge cake filled with blackberry jelly and lemon buttercream. An apple cake would also go down well. With any luck you'll catch some late summer sunshine!

Relaxed Chatty Tea

This is mainly a fantasy as, in the real world, all the people you would like to get together for tea and cakes and plenty of undisturbed talking one afternoon are all far too busy. You are probably far too busy yourself.

Anyway, in this fantasy, all your favourite friends are gathered together, without a care in the world, all chatting away and eating delicious cakes and drinking tea. You'll have all your best crockery out and there will be flowers on the table. No one will be on a diet or have a food allergy and no one will have to rush off. If there are any children in the party, they will be sweet and funny and behave beautifully and any babies will sleep peacefully, waking up occasionally to gurgle adorably for a few moments before snoozing off again.

Here are some suggestions as to what to serve in case you ever do manage to pull off such an event. You never know, it could happen – on a special birthday or anniversary perhaps!

You may just want to have tea and cakes or you may want some delicate little savouries as well. Make sure you provide your friends' favourite things but you may like to include some of the following:

- Delicate, crustless sandwiches cut into triangles – possibly **Egg and Cress, Smoked Salmon, Cucumber** or **Cream Cheese and Cucumber**
- Something chocolatey – a large **Chocolate Cake** to cut up, **Little Chocolate Cakes** or **Chocolate Butterflies** or **Brownie Buns**

- Something lemony – a large **Lemon Sponge** to cut up, **Lemon Drizzle Cake** or **Lemon Curd Tarts**
- Strawberries during the summer – either in little bowls with a jug of cream to pass round, or simply arranged on a plate with any larger ones cut in half, or **Strawberry Tarts**
- You may also like to include some **Scones**, already split and spread with jam and a dollop of cream, or possibly a few **Pastries** or some **Homemade Meringues**
- You can have a large pot of tea on the go: Earl Grey, perhaps, and put out an array of fruit or herb teas in the kitchen and let people make their own if they prefer something else.

Tea in the Garden

If you have a fairly secluded plot there is nothing nicer than tea in the garden on a summer's day: lazing around, with tea and cakes and cooling drinks, chatting to family and friends, the birds singing away in the background. Sometimes, during the darkest days of winter, you might imagine yourself having tea in the garden practically every day when summer finally comes. In reality, the weather can prevent you doing this very often at all, so at the very first sign of any sunshine in late spring get out there with your teapot and make the most of it!

Nursery Tea

The late Victorian and Edwardian eras were the golden age of Nursery Tea with Nanny. It conjures up a cosy picture of clean, happy children tucking into wholesome boiled eggs with soldiers and mugs of milk, a dappled grey rocking horse and a row of dolls and teddies not far away.

Before Queen Victoria came to the throne, childhood could be very short, and after babyhood children were often treated as young adults. Working-class children would work to help the family as best they could and children from more privileged backgrounds would be expected to adopt the manners of their elders. Whatever you feel about nursery life possibly being segregated from the rest of the household, at least it meant children were more able to be children: to have their own space to play and learn in and interesting toys and light-hearted books. Not all parents left their children with nannies all the time and Nursery Tea was often an opportunity for parents and children to be together.

Although Nursery Tea is an upper- and middle-class institution, the food has more in common with the working-class High Tea. It is the last meal of the day. This is a 'tea' where no actual tea is served: although Nanny and visiting parents would no doubt have taken the opportunity to have a cup of tea, the children would have drunk milk or water.

The children would have eaten a more substantial lunch and tea would be a lighter but still sustaining meal of something like boiled eggs and soldiers or bread and butter, little sandwiches (with the crusts left on, to make your hair curl), bread and butter and jam, buttered toast, currant buns and maybe a little cake or biscuit too.

Today, if we use the term at all, we just mean a meal at the end of the day for small children whose bedtime is still relatively early.

Children's Birthday Tea Party

Quite often a birthday party at home is for a fairly large group of very young children or a smaller group of older ones. Sometimes, for a few birthdays in between, children may go through a stage of preferring to be taken out for a 'treat' instead.

Younger children

Parties at home are great fun and always appreciated, but they can be hard work. Young children probably won't actually eat a great deal. They will be too excited to concentrate on very much food and can be heart-breakingly fussy, so don't knock yourself out by going overboard. Try to aim for a ratio of three quarters savoury to a quarter sweet and keep it fairly simple. Remember, homemade food is far better for young digestive systems than mass-produced stuff full of additives. Also you definitely don't want a houseful of toddlers high on junk food to contend with! If you are aiming to eat halfway through the party, have some drinks on hand from early on as children can get very thirsty if there is a lot of activity going on.

Don't forget the hungry mums and dads!
Parents often stay at parties for younger children and since parties are normally held over the lunch, or tea-time period, parents will be feeling a bit peckish themselves, so make sure you have made enough to feed them as well.

Suggestions include:
- **Little Sausages on Sticks** (avoid sticks for very young children)
- **Easy Sausage Rolls**
- **Little Cheese Tarts**
- **Sandwiches**: cut the crusts off and cut into four. Thinly sliced cheese, wafer thin ham, egg mayonnaise, Marmite, and jam, honey or marmalade all go down well with younger children
- **Cheesy Biscuits**
- **Toasted Cheese**
- Salady bits, grapes, strawberries
- Bread sticks are popular and not as salty and fatty as crisps. Lightly salted taco chips are also appreciated

As well as the birthday cake you can also have a selection of biscuits and small iced cakes and buns available. Most mums and dads agree: it is usually better to bring out the cakes after most of the savouries have been eaten!

Older children
Older children, on the other hand, can get very hungry indeed and eat an enormous amount. Popular choices might be a big pot of chilli or curry with plenty of rice, lasagne, shepherd's pie, spaghetti bolognese, homemade pizza, homemade hamburgers with plenty of salad and relishes, toasted sandwiches or piles of sausages and mash.

Crusty bread or garlic bread on the side is usually a good idea as are bowls of salad, grapes and taco chips.

Ice cream is usually a good choice for afterwards and it's nice to have the traditional birthday cake with candles. Alternatively, you might have a chocolate cake or a pyramid of fairy cakes or even brownies (try the **Chocolate Brownie Buns**) with candles stuck in them.

✓ **A note on plates**
Paper plates can be a bit flimsy and food can slide off too easily, especially in the hand of an excited toddler. It's better if you can to lay in a stock of cheerful coloured plastic plates that you can wash and use again and again for parties, picnics and in the garden.

If you are having a themed party and are hankering after novelty paper plates, what you can do instead is have plain plastic re-usable plates, as above, but buy coloured and patterned paper napkins.

A note on allergies and health issues
This may sound obvious, but do make sure you know all about any allergies that some of your small guests may have, particularly if parents aren't staying. Also, if someone suffers from asthma, for example, be sure his or her inhaler is available and that they are able to use it. Plus, of course, with very young children whose parents aren't staying, be sure to have a contact phone number. Young children can get very excited at parties and conditions normally well under control can be exacerbated by all the fun.

Christmas Tea and Christmas Holiday Teas
On Christmas day itself, all you may want to do at tea time is collapse into a chair with a cup of tea and a modest slice of Christmas cake, possibly followed a little later by a satsuma.

Since the Christmas holiday, strictly speaking, lasts for 12 days, only *beginning* on Christmas day, there will be plenty of other opportunities for festive teas. Here are a few suggestions to bear in mind over the holiday period:

- **Christmas Cake**
- **Mince Pies**
- **Little Treacle Tarts**
- **Rich, Dark, Moist Ginger Cake**
- **Gingerbread Biscuits**
- **Little Sausages on Sticks**
- **Easy Sausage Rolls**
- Cold Cuts – served with plenty of fresh salad or in sandwiches
- **Strawberry Jam**, served with Greek yoghurt, possibly sweetened and flavoured with a little sugar and vanilla
- Satsumas and walnuts – more fruit, in the form of grapes and highly polished fragrant Cox's Orange Pippins would also be welcome

Easter Tea

Easter is such a lovely time of year: the weather is starting to look a bit hopeful, the flowers are putting on a good show, birds are tweeting and lambs are gambolling in the fields. Easter Sunday is a good time to have family and friends round for tea in the afternoon and with none of the pressures of Christmas entertaining!

Eggs and fresh greenery are topical, so dainty egg or egg and cress sandwiches would work well, and possibly some baby quiches served with some spring salad leaves on the side. Hot cross buns, although strictly speaking meant for Good Friday, make a welcome bridge from the savoury part of the tea to the sweet.

You could make some iced **Fairy Cakes** and decorate them with sugar-coated mini-eggs or with some spring flowers from the garden: arrange them on the cakes just before serving. Stick with something you know is harmless such as primroses, pansies or violas. Sit them on kitchen paper first for a while if they are a bit damp and inspect closely for insect life. Be sure not to use anything that has been sprayed or is close to an exhaust-fume laden road.

You may like to have some **Easter Biscuits** as well, either cut in the traditional fluted round shape or into Easter chicks, eggs and bunnies.

A **Simnel Cake** could be your main cake. Even though originally it used to be eaten on Mothering Sunday, it seems to have become more of an Easter tradition. You could decorate it with the traditional 11 balls of marzipan or with some fresh flowers, as suggested for the **Fairy Cakes** – or you could do both!

Christening Party

Christenings are usually held in the morning, so you are probably more likely to have a lunch rather than a tea-time meal, but if you are having an informal buffet-style gathering and a christening cake at home, it can seem a bit more like a tea.

In any event, christenings are happy joyful occasions, with the emphasis on new life, children and families. There is likely to be a complete mix of age ranges, from the youngest baby to the most senior grandparent and all ages in between. Consequently, there needs to be a mix of food to appeal right across the age range whilst still keeping everything fairly simple (to keep preparation and clearing up to manageable levels).

If the party is held during the summer, the weather is fine and you have enough space, it's nice to be able to go into the garden. It's quite a good idea to set the food and drink up inside the house so that people can come in and choose what they want and take it outside. This way the food is protected from extremes of weather and it's easier to clear up afterwards. This also hopefully leaves the house itself fairly free for any older relatives to have a quiet sit down and for any very young children and babies to be settled down for a nap.

Drinks

You will probably want to serve champagne or something similar plus tea and coffee, juices and soft drinks, with possibly sherry for older guests. One bottle of champagne for every four or five guests should be ample for a christening tea, unless you are going for a full-blown 'wetting the baby's head' version, in which case, you'll need to allow a bit more. Unless you have a huge amount of people at the party, one bottle of sherry, with a second tucked away in reserve, should be plenty.

The christening cake

A fruit cake, covered with marzipan and icing, like a Christmas or wedding cake is the most traditional. Some people may have followed the old tradition of keeping the top tier of their wedding cake for the christening of their first child. If this is the case, the icing may have yellowed slightly; if this is the case, a professional cake decorator should be able to take off the old icing and replace it with sparkling fresh white icing.

If no one is very keen to have a fruit cake, you could have a chocolate one but it can get very messy if there are lots of children. One good idea is to have a pile or tower of **Fairy Cakes**. This looks really lovely, is usually very popular with children and adults, and there is no nerve-wracking and time-consuming slicing involved. If you want to go mad you could always put a few (not too many) celebratory candles on the top few cakes.

Food

Lots of little sandwiches usually appeal to all ages, and other savouries that can mainly be eaten with one hand are welcome. Little quiches, **Sausage Rolls** and individual pork pies are usually good. Salady bits such as cut up sticks of celery, red and yellow pepper, cucumber, carrot and cherry tomatoes (cut in half, otherwise they can be a bit squirty) are all welcome. It's nice to have little cubes of cheese and so on, on sticks, but if there are a lot of mobile toddlers in the party, it's best to do without the actual sticks to avoid accidents. Bread sticks and crispy things are usually popular, also olives and cocktail onions. Have some mayonnaise and mustard on the table.

Cakes and sweet things

Iced **Fairy Cakes** and **Butterfly Cakes** are always popular and look pretty. If it is summer you could set out little individual bowls of strawberries with spoons and provide sugar and cream. Fruity ice lollies are good for children – you could hand them out in plastic drinking cups (with the wrappers already removed if they are bought ones). A few little pastries as well are nice, and are popular with older guests.

Farewell Teas

At some time, or several times, in our lives we may need to arrange a funeral tea for a dear friend or relation. This is never easy: if the person who has died has lived a long and happy life, it is just about bearable and can even turn into a joyful celebration of a life well-lived, but if it is for a younger person it is hard to find any kind of consolation anywhere.

As with arranging the funeral service itself, planning the refreshments that follow can give a focus to the first stunned days of grief and is a specific task that can be done in honour of the deceased. The lunch or tea is an important continuation of the funeral as it creates an opportunity for everyone to be together to talk about the person who has died and to comfort each other.

There are several points to bear in mind when arranging such an occasion.

Some people may be so distraught or in such a state of shock that they may be unable to eat anything much at all. They may also feel very parched or faint. Have plenty of cool water and glasses available.

Other people may have travelled long distances, missed meals and may actually be ravenously hungry and in need of nourishment. It is particularly important for people who have travelled long distances and are driving to have something inside them, to revive them and keep them going on the journey back. Older relatives, who perhaps wouldn't normally travel very far, may have made a special effort and need particular consideration. Equally, there may be children in the party who will need to be catered for.

Usually, at a funeral tea, people won't be sitting down at a table but taking a plate of food and sitting somewhere else or just standing. Therefore, the food must be easy to pick up and to eat with one hand. It also needs to be fairly compact and neat (no oozing cream cakes or overfilled egg sandwiches) as people will most likely be wearing their best clothes and trying to talk to other guests: they need food they can pick up and eat neatly.

Another practical point to consider is where the tea is to be held. If it is in your home or a fully equipped hall with access to a fridge the choice of food will be wider. If the tea is going to be laid out sometime beforehand, particularly if the weather or indoor temperature is warm, you must avoid anything that is likely to spoil and become a breeding ground for bacteria. In this latter case, cold meats, smoked salmon and so on are completely out of the question.

The food needs to be nourishing but easy to digest and there should be plenty of reviving hot tea and coffee, jugs of cold water and juice available.

It's good to have sherry or something similar for a toast but, as this is a tea rather than a wake, alcohol probably won't figure much more largely than that: people may be driving or just not feel like drinking much. Older guests in particular, however, might appreciate a little tot of whisky or brandy or something similar in their tea. If you feel that might be the case, have a bottle standing by.

Sandwiches, savouries and cakes

It can be a nice idea to include, if it's practical, some of the deceased's favourite foods. Alternatively, this may be unbearably poignant and, if so, it's best not to. Traditionally, you might provide something like ham sandwiches, cheese sandwiches made with thinly sliced cheese, smoked salmon sandwiches and lightly filled egg mayonnaise sandwiches.

This may be sufficient along with some cake or you may like to add some more savouries such as baby quiches, little **Sausage Rolls** or miniature Melton Mowbray pork pies, cut in half. You might like to add a small amount of salad already prepared in bite-sized pieces, such as small leaves of lettuce, slices of cucumber cut in half, halved cherry tomatoes or quartered larger ones and so on. You could also provide some mustard and possibly some mayonnaise.

Buttered buns or buttered slices of fruit loaf, fruit cake, sponge cake, little iced cakes and **Jam Or Lemon Curd Tarts** are all good choices.

If the funeral is just before lunch and more seats are available, something more substantial may be called for. A ploughman's-style lunch can work well, provided keeping the food fresh and cool is no problem. The sight of some attractively laid out cold meats and cheeses, fresh bread and butter, salads and relishes can sometimes lift everyone's spirits a little. As well as the traditional crusty baguette-type bread, provide some softer rolls as well, particularly if older people and young children are present. Also, for those who have no appetite for anything hearty, include tea and coffee and biscuits.

Simple tea and cakes

If all the guests are very local, and the funeral is in the afternoon, you may prefer to have just tea and cakes. If there are any bakers among the proposed guests, they will in all likelihood be only too pleased to make a cake to contribute, so don't be afraid to ask beforehand. It's nice to involve other people as they are often desperate to help but don't quite know what to do, and it also spreads the load a bit.

Tea and biscuits

Sometimes, the immediate family will want to be alone after the service but there may be a wider group of guests not included in this, who may be longing for a restorative cup of tea and a chance to talk. What you can do in this situation is to arrange for tea and biscuits to be served after the service whilst the immediate family slip away. This can be arranged in a local community hall, church or village hall, or some churches have a specific refreshments area within the church building. Nobody will mind if there is no family representative present. Ask a friend or neighbour to take care of this, or someone from the church may be able to help. The family can then have something at home in private.

2. Sandwiches

Tea-time sandwiches are dainty, delicate little morsels rather than a substantial meal in themselves like a lunch-time or a breakfast sandwich. Traditionally, the crusts are cut off, and each round of sandwiches is cut into four: triangles are the classic way but you can also cut them into appetising little squares or fingers.

Which bread?
It's important to have *really* fresh bread for sandwiches: anything the *slightest* bit dry makes a very disappointing sandwich indeed.

Brown and white bread are both good choices for tea-time sandwiches but anything wholegrain usually seems a bit too hearty for the tea table. Some fillings seem to go better with white bread – egg mayonnaise, for example – others, such as smoked salmon, are a natural partner for brown. A lovely soft milk loaf works well with sweeter fillings such as jam or lemon curd. If you are making several varieties of sandwich, use both brown and white bread for variety.

Which spread?
The idea is to spread the bread with something that will contribute to the flavour and also waterproof the bread so that any moist fillings don't make it soggy. Equally, something like a single slice of meat can be a little dry without something spread on the bread first.

Butter gives the best flavour and mayonnaise can work well with certain fillings. The fun can go out of making sandwiches quite quickly if you are trying to spread butter straight from the fridge, so either soften it by putting it in the microwave for about 20 seconds or use one of the butters available that are mixed with a little oil and spread much more easily – take it out of the fridge for half an hour or so beforehand unless the weather is very hot as it can still be a little firm when it's fridge-cold.

Making lots of sandwiches

Making sandwiches can be a bit of a logistical nightmare if you have quite a few to make and several different fillings. Here are a few pointers to help make it as painless as possible.

Bear in mind that people usually make too many sandwiches, and there are usually some left over, so don't go overboard. If you are serving a variety of other foods as well, one round per person (four little sandwiches) is usually ample, as some people won't eat as many as that and the hungrier eaters can then take more than their share.

It's better to err on the side of caution and not do quite enough and then, if possible, be prepared to make another couple of rounds later should the need arise.

Make the sandwiches as close to the time of eating as you can so they are really fresh. Once they are made, arrange them on the serving plates and cover with foil, tucking it under the plates to secure: foil will keep the sandwiches fresh and you can remove it carefully afterwards and re-use it. You can soon drive yourself mad with cling film as it sticks everywhere except where you want it!

If there is going to be a slight delay and the room is warm, make sure any sandwiches filled with meat or fish are kept in the fridge. You may need to 'rationalise' your fridge in readiness beforehand.

Whatever your feelings about sliced bread normally, you can't beat having ready-sliced bread if you are making lots of sandwiches. Also, make sure the butter isn't hard (see previous page).

Before you start, make sure your working area is completely clear and you have plenty of elbow room.

Make one kind of sandwich at a time: butter the bread, put in the filling, stack them up no higher than four rounds at a time, remove the crusts and put them aside (see next page), cut the stack in four, arrange on the plates and cover.

Clear the fillings away from that batch and then move on to the next.

Sometimes, it can seem like a good idea for several of you to have a kind of production line going: one butters the bread, one does the fillings and so on. This *can* work but often, unless you are working in a very large kitchen, you may prefer to take it in turns to make a batch each from start to finish instead, as it's very easy to start falling over each other in a smaller kitchen!

One slight exception to this is if you are making a large number of egg sandwiches: it's much easier if one person has the single responsibility for shelling the eggs and preparing them.

What to do with all those crusts?
What do you do with all the crusts you've removed? If you are cutting the crusts off quite a few rounds of sandwiches the wastage can be quite alarming but don't worry, they do have a use.

Just put all the crusts onto a flat tray out of the way somewhere and cover lightly with a clean tea towel or greaseproof paper to allow them to dry out a little.

1. When you have a moment, break up the crusts into smaller pieces and whiz them in batches in the food processor to make breadcrumbs. Store in a plastic bag or box in the freezer. Take out what you need each time and reseal. They are useful for stuffings and coatings or to add to meatballs. You can also fry them in a little butter or oil and scatter over pasta dishes.

2. Alternatively, snip your crusts into small pieces with sharp kitchen scissors to make croutons and store in a plastic bag or box in the freezer. Take out what you need each time and reseal. These are very handy for scattering over savouries, salads and pasta dishes or even for a quick lunch with baked beans instead of toast.

To make croutons, heat some oil in a pan and spread a single layer of croutons across the bottom. Turn and coat in the oil and then lower the heat to moderate. Fry, turning occasionally, and keeping an eye on them, until they are crisp and golden.

Sandwich Fillings

Amazing Cheese Spread

Make delicate little cheese sandwiches with brown or white bread, a light smear of butter and a fairly generous layer of **Original Cheddar Spread**. If you have any herbs in the garden, a few snipped chives or a little chervil work well scattered over the spread.

Anchovy Paste

The homemade **Anchovy Paste** makes an excellent sandwich: delicate in appearance, yet robust in flavour. Use brown bread, real butter and spread thinly. You may like to add some very thinly sliced, peeled cucumber (see **Cucumber** Sandwiches).

Banana

You can make banana sandwiches with mashed banana for small children – don't fill them too full – but normally it's better to slice the banana. Thinly sliced brown or white bread, spread with real butter, and some fairly thinly sliced banana make a great sandwich. Make them just before you want to eat them to avoid the banana going soggy and brown.

Banana and Honey

As above but spread one slice of buttered bread with honey: set honey or runny honey both work well.

Thinly Sliced Roast Beef with Horseradish or Mustard

Butter some brown or white bread, or this may be a rare tea-time occasion for granary bread, and spread one slice with a light dab of horseradish sauce or mustard. Add the thinly sliced roast beef and serve with some delicate cocktail gherkins and silverskin onions.

Homemade Potted Beef

Spread homemade **Potted Beef** fairly generously on white or brown buttered bread. Some people may like to add a little trace of mustard. Again, some cocktail gherkins and silverskin onions would be welcome.

Cheese

When making a cheese sandwich, especially for tea time, slice the cheese *very* thinly into wafers – either with a sharp knife, one of those hand-held cheese slicers or use the slicing side of a box grater. It's much nicer to have several overlapping delicate little wafers of cheese rather than one great thick wedge.

Miniature Cheese

Make delicate little cheese sandwiches with brown or white bread, lightly buttered and filled with wafer thin cheese, as above. Cut the crusts off and cut each round into nine little squares. This makes them very appealing for children. Alternatively, make some using brown bread and some using white. Spear three sandwiches on a cocktail stick to make little nibbles, alternating the brown and white bread.

Cucumber

Cucumber sandwiches are the classic afternoon tea sandwich. Prepare the cucumber properly by peeling it first and then cutting it into wafer thin slices. Lay the slices on a double thickness of kitchen paper and sprinkle lightly with salt – a light grinding of Maldon Salt is perfect. Lay a couple more layers of kitchen paper on top and leave for a while. This draws out excess moisture from the cucumber and adds to the flavour.

Sandwich between slices of soft white bread, lightly buttered, and be sure to cut the crusts off and cut the sandwiches into dainty little triangles!

Thinly Sliced Cheese and Cucumber

Cheese and cucumber go beautifully together. Prepare the cucumber and slice the cheese thinly as previous recipe. Sandwich together in the same way. Mayonnaise, spread on the bread instead of butter, works well with cheese and cucumber if you fancy a change.

Thinly Sliced Roast or Poached Chicken with Maldon Salt and Mango Chutney

Butter some brown or white bread and cover with thinly sliced chicken. Grind a little Maldon Salt lightly over the top and dab on a little mango chutney: the kind made with smaller pieces of mango works better.

Plain Chicken and Maldon Salt

Sometimes, all you want is a perfectly plain chicken sandwich with just the *lightest* sprinkling of salt. Make as above but without the mango chutney.

Chicken, Lemon Mayonnaise and Watercress

Spread some brown bread lightly with mayonnaise into which you have stirred some very finely grated lemon zest and a small squeeze of juice. Cover with the thinly sliced chicken and add some sprigs of fresh watercress.

Cold Sausage Picnic Sandwich

These are fantastic eaten in the open air. Cook some really good butcher's sausages the day before, cool quickly and refrigerate. To make the sandwiches, slice the bread (brown or white) more thickly than usual for tea-time sandwiches, and butter. Slice each sausage lengthways: either in half or try to cut three thin slices. Lay between the slices of bread and cut each one in half. Take brown sauce and mustard with you; the ones in squirty bottles and jars are useful.

Cream Cheese or Cream Cheese and Cucumber

You may like to butter some brown or white bread very lightly first or you may prefer to spread the cream cheese directly onto the bread.

Cucumber goes beautifully with cream cheese. Prepare the cucumber as for **Cucumber** Sandwiches, and lay on top of the cream cheese.

Cream Cheese with Garden Herbs

Fresh garden herbs work well with cream cheese: snipped chives and/or chervil are excellent.

Egg Mayonnaise

Most people are partial to a classic egg mayonnaise sandwich. Don't over-boil the eggs and then leave them sitting in the cooling water, as they will be as rubbery and bouncy as little balls with nasty dark rings and a noticeably unpleasant smell! Boil for the time suggested below and then whip them out and get them into cold water as fast as you can.

To hard boil the eggs: bring the water to a fast boil and add the eggs once the water is boiling, and then set the timer and boil for 7–8 minutes *only*. Remove from the heat *immediately* and plunge into cold water. Roll the boiled eggs briskly on a flat surface and peel off the shell.

Don't forget: use eggs that are several days old for hard boiling, as if they are very fresh they are a nightmare to peel – you'll find yourself peeling away chunks of white with the shell.

Once they are cool, chop roughly with a sharp knife and then mash with a dinner fork, adding just enough mayonnaise to bind them together – you don't need a huge amount. You might find it easier to work on a board rather than using a dish: you can get a better angle with the fork on a board and it's a lot simpler.

Lightly spread some white bread (which is more traditional), or brown if you prefer, with either butter or mayonnaise and spread with the egg mixture – don't go mad with the filling as it can all drop out again when some unwary person tries to eat it.

Egg and Cress

Proceed as above but snip some old fashioned cress from a punnet (or grow your own) into the sandwich on top of the egg.

Lightly Curried Egg Mayonnaise

Make as for **Egg Mayonnaise** but stir a small amount of curry paste or curry powder into the mayonnaise before you mix it with the egg.

Homemade Fish Paste

Any of the homemade **Fish Pastes** make great sandwiches, either on their own or with some thinly sliced cucumber. Butter the bread lightly first.

Ham

Home-baked ham, cut as thinly as possible, or ready-cut wafer thin ham, are the best choices for a tea-time sandwich. If everybody likes mustard, spread a little lightly over one of the buttered slices of bread; if not, offer mustard separately.

Ham and Cheese

Wafer-thin ham and wafer-thin cheese together make a good sandwich.

Ham and Marmalade

This may sound a bit strange, but it's a great combination and works particularly well eaten in the open air as part of a picnic. If you are fond of mustard, a dab of English or wholegrain goes beautifully with both the ham and the marmalade.

Potted Ham

The homemade **Potted Ham** makes a good sandwich. Butter brown or white bread and spread the potted ham fairly generously. Again, a dab of mustard works well. Tiny cocktail gherkins and silverskin onions are appropriate for the tea table but feel free to take the full-size versions on a picnic.

Honey

Lovely, soft fresh bread, brown or white, spread with butter and honey make a welcome sandwich for a child or an adult. Both set and runny honey work well but, for some reason, runny is usually more popular with children. Eat with a banana for a picnic tea.

Jam

This is a classic child's sandwich, or one for nostalgic adults. Soft, very fresh white bread such as milk loaf works really well. Strawberry jam is the classic choice but also try apricot conserve, raspberry seedless jam or a jelly such as crab-apple or bramble.

Lemon Curd

This is more popular with older children or adults. A sandwich made with really fresh white bread and homemade lemon curd is so delicious, you won't need any cake!

Marmalade

Marmalade sandwiches are not just for well-known bears. If you have some really fresh white bread and are packing a quick picnic, marmalade sandwiches are a good thing to take if you haven't much in the way of cake or biscuits in the house. Generally speaking, a lighter marmalade with thin shreds of peel works best, but it's really a question of personal taste – you might prefer a granary bread with chunky marmalade. Whichever you choose, don't skimp on the butter.

Marmite, Marmite and Cheese, and Marmite and Lettuce

If you are a Marmite fan, there is nothing easier and tastier than a Marmite sandwich. Brown or white bread both work well, and don't skimp on the butter. *Do* skimp on the Marmite, however, and spread it nice and thinly.

A tiny smear spread over one buttered half of a cheese sandwich works well, and Marmite and crisp fresh lettuce are a wonderful combination. Why not go mad and have Marmite, Cheese *and* Lettuce!

Sand Sandwiches

These aren't really made from sand, of course, but brown sugar! Butter some very fresh bread, brown or white, making sure the butter isn't too soft but still quite 'shiny'. Sprinkle fairly lightly with soft brown sugar and cover with another buttered slice. Leave the crusts on and cut into two or four. These are popular as an occasional treat for children and nostalgic adults.

Smoked Salmon

If you are pushing the boat out, this is the sandwich to serve. Thinly cut, lightly buttered, fresh brown bread, delicious smoked salmon with possibly the *lightest* touch of freshly ground black pepper, served in little triangles garnished with wedges of lemon. Perfect. If it's a really special occasion, you can pretend you are at the Ritz and treat yourselves to a glass of champagne as well!

Alternative Smoked Salmon

Make as above but instead of butter, spread the bread with mayonnaise – don't go mad with it but don't be too mean either. Add a touch of freshly ground black pepper and garnish with lemon, as before.

Smoked Salmon, Cream Cheese and Black Pepper

This is the sandwich version of the classic bagel filling. Spread brown bread lightly with butter or just with the cream cheese, grind a little black pepper lightly over the top and add the smoked salmon. Serve with wedges of lemon.

Smoked Salmon with a Touch of Horseradish Sauce

Admittedly, this sounds strange but it works really well: the flavours complement each other beautifully. Spread brown bread lightly with butter and dab a little horseradish sauce on one side, then add the smoked salmon. Serve with wedges of lemon.

Tinned Salmon

Tinned salmon, pink or red, makes a great sandwich. Drain the liquid from the salmon, mash with a fork and bind together with a little mayonnaise – alternatively, if you are going down the nostalgia route, use a dab of salad cream.

A little squeeze of lemon juice and a light grinding of black pepper are nice additions to the salmon and mayonnaise mixture.

Sandwich between brown bread – either lightly buttered or lightly spread with mayonnaise. This is good just as it is or with some thinly sliced cucumber. As with egg mayonnaise: don't overfill.

Tinned Tuna

Drain the liquid from the tuna, mash with a fork and bind together with a little mayonnaise. Add a little squeeze of lemon juice and a light grinding of black pepper. Sandwich between brown bread – either lightly buttered or lightly spread with mayonnaise. This is good just as it is or with some thinly sliced cucumber. As above: don't overfill.

Tuna and Cottage Cheese

This sounds *extremely weird* but tastes surprisingly good! Mix together equal quantities of drained, mashed tuna and cottage cheese. Sandwich between lightly buttered brown bread.

Flavoured Butters

You can make flavoured butter very easily and use it to add an extra special touch to sandwiches. Choose the butter to complement the filling.

- **Lemon Butter**: Stir a little finely grated lemon zest into softened butter and use with fish, chicken and salady fillings.

- **Curry Butter**: Stir a little curry powder or curry paste into softened butter and use with egg, plain chicken or beef, tuna or salad.

- **Chilli Butter**: Stir a little curry powder or finely chopped fresh chilli into softened butter and use with cheese, plain chicken, beef or sausage.

- **Herb Butter**: Stir some finely chopped or snipped 'soft' herbs, such as chives, chervil, mint, parsley, dill or French tarragon, into softened butter and use with egg, cheese, cream cheese or chicken.

3. Savouries

Little Sausages on Sticks

It can be quite difficult to find really good cocktail sausages. Instead, buy good quality chipolatas and gently squeeze each one in the middle and twist to make two smaller sausages, and then cut them apart with kitchen scissors. Bake in an un-greased baking dish, at 180°C (fan oven) or equivalent, for approximately 20 minutes, turning halfway.

When cooked prick each sausage gently to release surplus fat and drain on kitchen paper. Spear with cocktail sticks and serve with a selection of mustards.

Little Cheese Tarts

For the pastry
160g (6oz) plain flour
40g (1½oz) butter, cold and cut into small pieces
40g (1½oz) block vegetable shortening, cold and cut into small pieces
Pinch of salt
2–3 tablespoons cold water

For the filling
1 small onion, plus a little oil for frying
75g (3oz) cheese
1 egg
1 egg yolk
Pinch of dry mustard powder
Freshly ground black or white pepper
6 tablespoons cream (single or double)

You will need a greased 12-cup tart tin and a 6cm (2½in) plain
cutter.

1. Preheat the oven to 180°C (fan oven) or equivalent.

2. Sieve the flour into the processor and add the butter, vegetable
shortening and salt. Whiz into fine crumbs. Add the water and whiz
again. Once it is starting to form big crumbs and clump together, turn
it out onto a lightly floured board and knead it gently into a ball.

3. Roll it gently with a lightly floured rolling pin and cut into rounds.
Press them gently into the tart tin.

4. Peel and slice the onion fairly finely. Fry until soft and barely
coloured. Drain on kitchen paper. Grate the cheese.

5. Beat the egg and egg yolk gently together with the mustard powder
and pepper. Add the cream and whisk in lightly until smooth.

6. Spread the onion evenly over the bottom of the pastry case and pour
the cream and egg mixture over the top. Finally, scatter the cheese evenly
over the surface. Bake for 15 minutes or until risen and until golden.
Serve warm or cold.

Little Cheese and Bacon Tarts

Make these in exactly the same way as the **Little Cheese Tarts**
(above) but also fry 2 or 3 rashers of lean bacon, cut into small
squares or matchsticks. Add a little oil to the pan if necessary. The
bacon should be cooked through but not crisp. Drain on kitchen
paper and scatter over the base of the flan with the onion.

Spoon the filling into the unbaked cases, as above, and bake for
around 12–15 minutes or until the pastry is cooked and the filling is
risen and golden. Eat warm or cold.

Easy Sausage Rolls

Instead of fiddling around with sausage meat, buy good quality butcher's sausages and readymade, ready-rolled, all-butter puff pastry: preferably Dorset Pastry.

Quantities to suit of:
Good quality butcher's sausages
Good quality all-butter, ready-rolled, frozen puff pastry, defrosted in the fridge until pliable

1. You will need a large, greased baking tray.

2. Preheat the oven to 200°C (fan oven) or equivalent.

3. Roll each sausage in a blanket of pastry and cut from the roll with a sharp knife, brush along the cut end with a little water and seal the edge. Lay each sausage roll join-side down on the prepared tray. Make 2 or 3 little slits with the point of a sharp knife along the length.

4. For delicate little bite-sized sausage rolls, cut each pastry-rolled sausage into four with a sharp knife and make a couple of slits in the top.

5. Bake on a greased baking tray for approximately 20 minutes until puffed and golden.

You may also like to brush the sausage rolls with an egg beaten with a teaspoon of water, before they go into the oven, for a glossy professional finish.

Savoury Garden Tarts with All-Butter Pastry

These elegant summery tartlets are just right for a light high tea in the garden. Serve with a leafy salad, some boiled new potatoes and fresh bread and butter. The recipe below will give you your foundation. You can then top the light, cheesy, savoury custard with a few extra vegetables, either from the garden or whatever you happen to have in the fridge.

Suggestions – use singly or mix together:

- Asparagus – thin spears or fatter ones sliced vertically
- A few fresh peas or small mange tout
- Baby spinach leaves, torn slightly and incorporated into the savoury custard
- Small florets of broccoli
- Thinly sliced red or green pepper
- Baby sweetcorn – whole or sliced in half vertically – or sweetcorn kernels
- Light scattering of 'soft' herbs such as: chives, chervil, dill, basil or French tarragon

For the pastry
160g (6oz) plain flour
Pinch of salt
80g (3oz) butter, cold and cut into small pieces
2 tablespoons cold water

For the savoury custard
1 egg
1 egg yolk
Pinch of dry mustard powder
Freshly ground black or white pepper
6 tablespoons cream (single or double, but preferably not extra thick)

50g (2oz) cheese, grated
Plus: garden herbs and vegetables of your choice (see above)

You will need 6 greased, fluted, loose-bottomed 10cm (4in) tartlet tins, and a baking tray, plus baking beans (preferably ceramic) and greaseproof paper.

1. Preheat the oven to 180°C (fan oven) or equivalent.

2. Cut out 6 circles of greaseproof paper using one of the loose bottoms as a template, and put your baking beans into a jug with a good pouring spout for ease of use.

Making the pastry
3. Sieve the flour and salt carefully into the bowl of your food processor and add the butter. Whiz into fine crumbs. Add the water and whiz until the mixture is starting to come together. Turn it out onto a floured board and knead it lightly until it forms a ball.

4. Divide the pastry into 6 equal pieces.

5. Working with one piece at a time, form it into a ball and roll out gently, keeping it circular, on a very lightly floured board with a lightly floured rolling pin, to a thickness of just less than half a centimetre.

6. Drape the pastry circle over the prepared tin and lower gently into position. Firm the pastry lightly into the fluted sides and coax it into shape. Smooth your hand carefully over the top of the tin so the fluted edges cut through the excess pastry and trim it away or gently roll your rolling pin over the top.

7. It is really important that you don't stretch the pastry: if you do it will ping back down the sides of the tins during baking like over-stretched elastic!

8. For ease of use, arrange the tartlet tins on a baking tray. Put a little circle of greaseproof paper in each one and fill almost to the brim with baking beans.

9. Bake for 12–15 minutes or until crisp and golden.

10. Leave to settle and cool in the tin.

11. Once cool, remove the baking beans from the pastry cases. The easiest way is to pick up each pastry case and tip the beans out carefully into an empty washing up bowl or something similar. Peel away the greaseproof paper circles.

Making the savoury custard
12. Beat the egg and egg yolk gently together with the mustard powder (stir it through a tea strainer with a teaspoon to prevent it clumping together) and pepper. Add the cream and whisk in lightly.

13. Scatter the cheese over the base of each baked pastry case. Pour in the cream and egg mixture. Arrange your garden or fridge bits and pieces over the top.

14. Bake for 15 minutes or until risen and until golden. Serve warm or cold.

Using the pastry trimmings
Re-roll the trimmings and use them to make some little jam tarts. The re-rolled pastry is fine for small tarts but a little bit over-worked for anything larger.

Potted Ham

You don't come across potted ham very often these days but it is seriously nice. As well as tea time, it's great for a weekend lunch or supper. Try it in sandwiches, with crusty bread or rolls, or on hot buttered toast. Add possibly a dab of mustard and a crisp pickle (silverskin onion, gherkin or plain mixed pickles or piccalilli are all good) on the side. Some leafy green salad also goes well.

Instead of leftover ham, this recipe involves boiling a ham knuckle, which you can buy from your local butcher for about the same price, or a little less, than half a dozen eggs.

Ham knuckle, also known as ham hock, is the same cut as the one traditionally used for thick pea and ham soup. It is so delicious and affordable it is also worth cooking for the ham alone, which can be stripped from the bone using a dinner fork to produce succulent, thick shreds of meat, great for chunky sandwiches or served hot with a fried egg and some home-fried potatoes on the side.

SERVES 6

1 ham knuckle
1 large onion, sliced
1–2 carrots, peeled and cut into strips
2–3 sticks of celery, trimmed and cut into strips
1 bay leaf
A few black and/or white peppercorns
Clarified butter (optional)

You will need 6 small 7.5cm (3in) ramekins.

You may need to soak your ham knuckle overnight if it's very salty. Check with your butcher.

1. Put the ham into a large saucepan with the onion, carrot, celery,

bay leaf and peppercorns. Pour over enough water to cover: this will probably be about 3 litres (6 pints) or so. Bring to the boil, skim off any froth and simmer fairly briskly for 2 to 3 hours, or until the ham is virtually falling off the bone. Check from time to time, adding more water if necessary.

2. Once cooked, take the ham from the stock, cover with foil and leave to rest in a warm place for 20 minutes or so. Reserve the stock and keep in a cool place (not the fridge as it will be too hot at this stage).

3. Use a dinner fork to take all the ham off the bone, once it has rested. Remove and discard as much fat as you can: don't worry about the odd tiny bit here and there as it will add to the flavour and texture.

4. You should have about 225g (8oz) of meat or thereabouts. Put the meat into the food processor and add a couple of tablespoons of the stock or cooking water. Whiz and then add a couple more tablespoons of stock. Repeat until you have added about 10 tablespoons in all and the ham is the texture of smooth pâté and is slightly clumping together. Add a spot more stock if it seems too dry. You shouldn't need any further seasoning at all as the flavour is already delicious: you definitely won't need any salt and pepper.

5. Divide the mixture between 6 small 7.5cm (3in) ramekins. Alternatively, you can use 4 larger ramekins or 1 large dish or container: it doesn't have to be round; a rectangular one looks good, and white china looks particularly attractive against the rosy pink colour of the ham. Once the ham is all potted, take a teaspoon of the cooking liquid at a time and pour 1 teaspoonful over the surface of each ramekin of ham to add extra moisture: adjust quantities accordingly if you are using larger containers.

6. Cover with foil or cling film, or clarified butter, if using. Store in the fridge and use within 48 hours.

Clarified Butter

Clarified butter is very pure, clear, golden, melted butter that has been separated from the milk solids that butter contains. The solids are the part that burns and once they have gone, you can cook with the butter on a much higher heat. Ghee, which is used in Indian cooking, is unsalted butter that has been clarified or 'made clear'.

Unsalted butter is normally used for clarifying. This is only because once the butter is clarified some of the salt may be removed at the same time as the milk solids.

It's really easy to clarify butter – 225g (8oz) will give you enough clarified butter to seal your potted ham or potted beef with some left over for cooking. You can use slightly less if you like, say 175g (6oz), but don't go below that, or by the time you have removed all the solids you will have hardly anything left!

1. Cut the butter into small pieces.

2. Heat gently in a heavy-bottomed saucepan over low heat until it spits and cracks and bubbles.

3. Remove the pan from the heat and very carefully skim off the froth from the top with a tablespoon.

4. Pour the clear, golden liquid butter carefully through a nylon sieve into a container, taking care not to include the solids on the bottom of the pan. If you have some clean muslin or a brand new disposable dish cloth to line the sieve, so much the better. (It's tempting to just pour the whole lot through the sieve, but don't, because the milky solids will get through!)

5. Cool slightly and pour over your finished ramekins of potted ham

or beef. Store what's left, in the fridge in a clean jar with a lid, and use it for frying: it gives everything a beautiful flavour.

6. Always make sure it is stored covered in the fridge. Uncovered butter soon reacts with the air or oxidises and starts to taste 'stale' and 'airy'.

7. You can also freeze clarified butter.

Potted Beef

Like the **Potted Ham**, this is great in sandwiches, with crusty bread or rolls, or on hot buttered toast. Mustard and pickles, particularly piccalilli and gherkins, are all good served on the side, and some fresh, crisp salad also goes well. Chuck steak, blade or skirt, are all really economical cuts, and they respond well to long, slow cooking and are full of flavour.

SERVES 6

225g (8oz) chuck steak, blade or skirt (ask your local butcher)
A little oil, for frying
1 large onion, cut into 4
1–2 carrots, peeled and cut in half lengthways
2–3 sticks of celery, trimmed and cut in half lengthways
Approximately $^1/_2$ litre ($2^1/_2$pts) hot water
1 bay leaf
1–2 tablespoons Worcestershire sauce
1 level tablespoon soft dark brown sugar
A little salt
Clarified butter (optional)

You will need 6 small 7.5cm (3in).ramekins.

1. Brown the beef in the oil. Put the prepared vegetables into a clean pan and add the water, bay leaf, Worcestershire sauce and brown sugar. Stir and add the browned beef – including all of the beefy residue from the pan, so be sure to scrape it all off. Bring everything to the boil and then simmer gently, partially covered with a lid, for 2–3 hours until the beef is falling apart and very tender. Check from time to time, adding more water if necessary.

2. Once cooked, remove the pieces of beef from the stock, and transfer to a warm plate. Cover with foil and leave to rest in a warm place for 20 minutes or so. Strain and reserve the stock and keep in a cool place (not the fridge as it will be too hot at this stage).

3. Put the meat into the food processor and add a couple of tablespoons of the stock. Season very lightly with salt. Whiz and then add a couple more tablespoons of stock. Repeat until you have added about 10 tablespoons in all and the beef is a fairly smooth, pale paste and is slightly clumping together. Add a spot more stock if it seems too dry.

4. Check for seasoning: you may need the slightest touch more salt.

5. Divide the mixture between 6 small 7.5cm (3in) ramekins. Alternatively, you can use 4 larger ramekins or 1 large dish or container. Once the beef is all potted, take a teaspoon of the cooking liquid at a time and pour 1 teaspoonful over the surface of each ramekin of beef to add extra moisture: adjust quantities accordingly if you are using larger containers.

6. Once cold, cover with foil or cling film, or clarified butter, if using. Store in the fridge and use within 48 hours.

7. Once any remaining stock is cold, store in the fridge and use within 48 hours or freeze.

Original Cheddar Spread

This spread is just fabulous on toasted crumpets for a cosy Sunday tea tucked up in front of the fire on a winter's afternoon. It's also lovely on toast, on fresh bread and butter or on digestive biscuits. It is good as a dip with slices of celery or apple, although don't go too mad obviously, as it's quite rich. If you can lay your hands on a few chives try the spread on fresh bread and butter or a buttered roll with a few snipped chives on top.

110g (4oz) Cheddar cheese
1 tablespoon semi-skimmed milk
3–4 teaspoons rapeseed oil (or similar mild oil)

1. Cut the cheese into smaller pieces and whiz in the processor until it becomes rather bumpy grated cheese.

2. Add the milk and whiz briefly. Add a teaspoon of oil and whiz again. Add the rest of the oil and whiz until smooth.

Fish Pastes

All of the following fish pastes are fabulous spread on hot buttered toast with or without an extra squeeze of lemon. Alternatively, use in sandwiches or on buttered rolls, with possibly some thinly sliced cucumber. Each of the following recipes will make sufficient to fill, or almost fill, a large ramekin measuring 8.5cm (3½in) in diameter. You will need a food processor to make these fish pastes. Try them once and you'll be hooked!

Sardine and Tomato Paste

This paste is a bit like the loaves and the fishes: it seems to make a single tin of sardines go much further than usual. This recipe makes more than enough paste for two, whereas a tin of sardines on toast normally seems barely enough for one.

120g tin sardines in tomato sauce
2 teaspoons mild oil
Freshly ground black or white pepper to taste
Squeeze of lemon juice to taste

1. Empty the sardines and tomato sauce into the bowl of your food processor. Add the oil, pepper and lemon juice. Whiz until smooth, stopping a couple of times, and scrape the paste down from the sides of the bowl with a flexible spatula.

2. Check for seasoning. Refrigerate and use within 24 hours.

Tuna Paste

185g tin tuna in spring water, drained
2 teaspoons mild, flavourless oil
Freshly ground black or white pepper
2 teaspoons lemon juice – or to taste

1. Empty the tuna into the bowl of your food processor. Add the oil, pepper and lemon juice. Whiz until smooth, stopping a couple of times, and scrape the paste down from the sides of the bowl with a flexible spatula.

2. Check for seasoning. You may need a touch of salt. Refrigerate and use within 24 hours.

Tuna and Mayonnaise Paste

185g tin tuna in spring water, drained
2 teaspoons mayonnaise
Freshly ground black or white pepper
2 teaspoons lemon juice – or to taste

1. Empty the tuna into the bowl of your food processor. Add the mayonnaise, pepper and lemon juice. Whiz until smooth, stopping a couple of times, and scrape the paste down from the sides of the bowl with a flexible spatula.

2. Check for seasoning. Refrigerate and use within 24 hours.

Salmon Paste

You can use either pink or red salmon for this recipe.

212g tin salmon, drained
2 teaspoons mild, flavourless oil
Freshly ground black or white pepper
2 teaspoons lemon juice – or to taste

1. Empty the salmon into the bowl of your food processor. Add the oil, pepper and lemon juice. Whiz until smooth, stopping a couple of times, and scrape the paste down from the sides of the bowl with a flexible spatula.

2. Check for seasoning. Refrigerate and use within 24 hours.

Salmon and Mayonnaise Paste

This is lovely and luscious.

212g tin salmon, drained
2 teaspoons mayonnaise
Freshly ground black or white pepper
2 teaspoons lemon juice, or to taste

1. Empty the salmon into the bowl of your food processor. Add the mayonnaise, pepper and lemon juice. Whiz until smooth, stopping a couple of times, and scrape the paste down from the sides of the bowl with a flexible spatula.

2. Check for seasoning. Refrigerate and use within 24 hours.

What is the difference between red and pink salmon?
They are different species. Red Sockeye salmon is larger and more deeply flavoured than pink Humpy or Humpback salmon (which develops a hump on its back once it leaves the sea and swims upstream to spawn). Red salmon is not as plentiful as pink salmon so it has more rarity value, which is why it is more expensive.

Anchovy Paste

This isn't the most handsome and appetising of spreads to look at, but it tastes delicious and is fabulous spread thinly on hot buttered toast. The quantities given are for a very small amount but you won't need very much as it's rather powerful.

50g tin anchovies in oil
Squeeze of lemon juice
Tip of a teaspoon of cayenne pepper
Freshly ground black pepper

1. Whiz the anchovies, including their oil, and the lemon juice, cayenne and black pepper together in the food processor or pound together in a pestle and mortar. Alternatively, mash everything together with a dinner fork.

2. Once you have a smooth paste, transfer it to a small dish or ramekin, cover and store in the fridge. Serve spread thinly on triangles or wide soldiers of hot buttered toast.

Cheesy Biscuits

These are perfect for all kinds of parties and picnics. They are very similar to cheese straws but rolled and cut out as biscuits.

MAKES ABOUT 15 DEPENDING ON CUTTER SIZE

50g (2oz) plain flour
Pinch of dry mustard powder
Pinch of salt
25g (1oz) butter, softened
75–110g (3–4oz) grated well-flavoured Cheddar cheese

1. You will need a large, greased baking tray and some biscuit cutters.

2. Preheat the oven to 180°C (fan oven) or equivalent.

3. Sieve the flour and mustard powder carefully into the bowl of your food processor, sprinkle in the salt and add the butter. Give the mixture a quick whiz to start everything off and add the cheese (the lesser amount of cheese will make a slightly less rich biscuit, the greater amount will be a little cheesier and richer).

4. Keep whizzing, stopping from time to time to remove the lid and give the mixture a quick stir, until the mixture starts to clump together. Stop the machine, remove the blade and transfer the mixture to a clean board. Gently bring the mixture together with your hands and knead it lightly until it looks and feels like a ball of cheesy marzipan.

5. Flour the board lightly and, using a floured rolling pin, roll out the mixture to a thickness of just less than a centimetre. Cut out your shapes and arrange on the prepared tray. Re-roll and cut out the rest. If you have any dough left over, roll it into little balls and flatten with your hand or a fork and bake with the others.

6. Bake for 7–8 minutes, or until they are golden in colour. Remove from the oven and leave to settle for a few moments. Remove carefully with a palette knife and finish cooling on a wire rack. Store in an airtight tin.

Welsh Rarebit

Welsh Rarebit makes a lovely lunch, but it is just as good at tea time. Serve it as a high tea with some salad and a dollop of coleslaw or, for a more relaxed tea by the fire, cut it into triangles or wide fingers.

SERVES 1–2 BUT IT'S EASY TO DOUBLE OR TREBLE QUANTITIES

50g (2oz) mature Cheddar, grated
1 medium egg yolk
2 tablespoons semi-skimmed milk
Pinch of dry mustard or dab of English readymade mustard from a jar
Few shakes of Worcestershire sauce
2 slices of decent bread, brown or white, not too thickly cut
Butter for spreading

1. Combine the cheese, egg yolk, milk and seasoning in a small, heavy saucepan and cook on a medium heat, stirring pretty much all the time. It will thin down and then thicken slightly again as it amalgamates and starts to bubble gently. Don't take your eye off it or have the heat too high or the egg will split and scramble.

2. Once the cheese has melted and the mixture is smooth, take it off the heat and set aside: it will thicken even more. Lightly toast the bread and allow it to cool slightly before buttering: this is because the toast needs to be crisp to support the rarebit. Spread the cheese mixture onto the toast and grill until bubbling and golden.

3. You might like to try adding wholegrain mustard for a change: the flavour is good and the mustard seeds speckled through the rarebit look attractive.

Light and luscious version
This is possibly even more delicious than the original: instead of 2 tablespoons of milk, use a generous heaped tablespoon of half fat crème fraîche.

Blue cheese version
You can make Welsh Rarebit with blue cheese as well. It's particularly good just after Christmas if you have some Stilton or similar left over. Use blue cheese instead of the Cheddar. Be careful not to over-brown it under the grill though or the flavour will be ruined. Lovely with some cranberry sauce on the side, some green salad and a few walnuts.

Ham Rarebit

Lay a wafer-thin slice of ham onto the lightly buttered toast and top with the rarebit mixture. Finish off under the grill as usual.

Toasted Cheese

Toasted cheese is a real favourite with most people. Make sure the toast has cooled and crisped slightly before you put the cheese on top. Some people butter it first, some don't. Whether or not you butter the whole slice, it's nice to butter the edges of the toast so they crisp up nicely under the grill. A generous layer of grated cheese melts more evenly and satisfyingly than sliced, it also goes further.

Crumbly cheeses such as Cheshire, Wensleydale, Caerphilly and Lancashire all toast brilliantly and make a change from Cheddar.

Cheesy Chilli Crumpets

The chilli makes this into quite a bracing tea-time dish. Toast the crumpets and butter lightly. Arrange some grated cheese carefully on top and add a thin slice or two of red chilli. Put under a hot grill until golden and bubbling and the chilli is very slightly charred.

4. Cakes, Buns and Scones

The Secret of Cakes

Some of us feel very strongly that de-activated self-raising flour is a major cause of disappointing flat cakes. If you are using self-raising flour for a recipe it needs to be *completely fresh*. It should be well within its sell-by date and it also helps if the bag has not been opened for very long.

It must also be stored properly in a cool dry place. If you are wondering why years ago cakes seemed to rise more, it could be because more people had cool, dry pantries and larders then, and didn't keep their flour in a warm kitchen cupboard. Possibly also they baked more regularly and used their flour more quickly.

As self-raising flour can be unreliable and lose its raising ability so easily, it might be time to move away from it altogether and find a reliable alternative.

Instead of self-raising flour, you can use plain flour and add a raising agent to it yourself. Baking powder works well for cakes and biscuits that don't need a light fluffy rise, but you need something with a bit of extra oomph for light airy sponges and scones.

For the lighter cake recipes in this book I have used bicarbonate of soda and cream of tartar at a ratio of one part bicarbonate of soda to two parts cream of tartar: it works like magic!

Once you have sorted out the flour, you are well on your way to a successful cake but there are a few other factors to bear in mind as well.

Correct oven temperature and times

Ovens can very tremendously. Even the same oven can vary as it ages. Keep a note of the times and temperatures for your own oven that you have used for particular recipes. It's easiest just to pencil them in by the actual recipes in the recipe book. The notes will then be there for you to refer to when you make those recipes again.

It is worth noting here that fan ovens generally do seem hotter, as the hot air circulates round the food: the difference is usually about 20°C.

Eggs must be very fresh

As an egg gets older its composition changes and the components
that help the cake to rise deteriorate and eventually stop working. If
an egg pops out of the shell with a round yolk like a little ball it is
fresh; if it flops out looking very flat, it isn't.

Use warmed, softened butter

Unlike when making pastry, butter must be soft and slightly warm
for a successful cake mix. If you try to mix it in when it is cold and
too hard the cake will be heavy. An easy way to soften butter quickly
is to put it in the microwave on high for 20–30 seconds.

Use the right type of sugar

Unless the recipe specifically gives a choice, use the sugar type
specified. Caster sugar is best for light sponge cakes as it is much finer.

Correct mixing

Generally, with some notable exceptions such as muffins, cakes need
to be thoroughly mixed. However, this doesn't mean you should
over-mix: be thorough but don't *over do it*. Mix sponge cakes until
they look smooth and glossy, then ease the mixture gently into the
baking tin(s).

Even if you are using a food processor, try to add the ingredients
in the same stages you would if you were mixing by hand, rather than
the all-in-one method some people prefer. This means whiz the
butter and sugar together first until they are combined and fluffy,
then sieve a layer of flour over them, next add the eggs (already
beaten lightly with a fork). Finally add the rest of the flour and, after
a quick whiz, extra liquid, such as milk, if you are using any.

Sieve your flour

Modern flour is fine and light but it does settle in the bag and you
need to aerate it again. This is why you need to sieve it: to let lots of
air in so you end up with a light, well risen cake. Hold your sieve
quite a way above the bowl if you can.

Icing sugar, on the other hand, needs sieving to remove any lumps, so it is perfectly fine to push icing sugar through the sieve with a spoon, in fact positively *don't* sieve it in the same way as flour as it's much finer and you will be enveloped in clouds of choking sweet dust!

Correct size tins
You must use the same size tin as specified in the recipe. The cooking times have been worked out around a particular tin size so if you use something different it won't cook at the same rate.

Don't open the oven door whilst baking is in progress!
Every time you open your oven door, you lose heat. It is particularly crucial that you don't lose heat when you are baking something that needs to rise, such as a sponge cake. If you have a window in your oven door, make use of it to check on progress. If you do have to return a cake to the oven because it's not quite done, be aware that it won't be quite as good as if it had been undisturbed for the whole baking time and make a note for next time.

If you are embarking on cake baking for the first time, it's a good idea to start off with fairy cakes. They are much less scary as they almost always rise! Once you have built your confidence up you can then bake a large-size cake: you'll wonder what all the fuss was about!

A mountain of fairy cakes makes a perfect birthday cake for any age group. Pile them up and put a few candles on the top ones. They are much easier to serve as well: no slicing!

All Sorts of Fairy Cakes and Butterfly Cakes

The mixture is exactly the same as the sponge cake mixture and the same rules apply: it is best to have everything slightly warm so leave the eggs out of the fridge and warm the butter slightly in the microwave if necessary: 10–20 seconds or so on high is usually just about right.

Iced Fairy Cakes

You can have fun decorating these with whatever takes your fancy.

MAKES ABOUT 18 CAKES

175g (6oz) butter, softened
175g (6oz) unrefined caster sugar

175g (6oz) very fresh self-raising flour
or
175g (6oz) plain flour
2 level teaspoons cream of tartar
1 level teaspoon bicarbonate of soda

3 eggs
2 tablespoons milk

You will need a 12-cup muffin tin plus paper cases.

1. Preheat the oven to 180°C (fan oven) or equivalent.

2. Whiz the butter and sugar together in a food processor until combined and fluffy. Sieve in some of the flour, the cream of tartar and the bicarbonate of soda and add the eggs. Then sieve in the rest of the flour. Whiz again. Add the milk and whiz until smooth and

glossy. You may need to scrape the mixture down from the sides a couple of times with a flexible spatula.

3. Arrange the paper cases in the muffin tin and spoon 2 generous teaspoons of mixture into each case. Bake for around 15 minutes or until risen and pale golden and springy to the touch. A skewer or wooden cocktail stick should come out clean when inserted. Remove from the tin with a small palette knife and cool on a wire rack. Bake the remaining part batch. Decorate with **Glacé** or **Pink Icing**, below.

Note: This will give you muffin-shaped fairy cakes with rounded tops. If you want a flatter, more cup cake type size, fill each case barely halfway and once in the oven check after 12 minutes or so. You should have enough mixture left over for about another half dozen cakes.

Glacé Icing

The lemon juice takes the edge off the sweetness and if you use the glycerine it will give the icing a lovely, sticky, slightly stretchy quality.

225g (8oz) icing sugar
2 tablespoons lemon juice (sieve through a tea strainer)
2 teaspoons glycerine (optional)

1. Sieve the icing sugar into a large bowl and stir in the lemon juice and glycerine, if using. Beat with a wooden spoon until glossy.

2. Spoon over the cooled cakes. You can either spread the icing over the whole top of the cake, or spoon on a little circle of icing in the middle of each cake.

Pink Icing

For pink-tinted icing without using food colouring, add a little **sieved raspberry jam**. For a more lilac-toned pink, use a little touch of blackberry jelly or sieved blackcurrant jam.

Teeny Tiny Fairy Cakes

These are exactly the same but half the size. Make up the mixture and icing in exactly the same way but bake in two 12-cup mini muffin tins instead, and then a second batch, using petit four cases. They will take less time to bake, usually about 8–10 minutes.

Currant Fairy Cakes

Make up the fairy cake mixture, as page 56, and once it is all mixed together remove the processor blade and stir in **75–110g (3–4 oz) of currants** (depending on how curranty you want them).

These are lovely plain but possibly even better iced with **Glacé Icing** page 57.

Butterfly Cakes

These little cakes look so pretty and delicate. Make up the fairy cake mixture, as page 56, filling the cases half full. Make up some **Lemon Buttercream**, below.

Once the cakes are cool, slice the tops off and put to one side. Spoon a little dollop of buttercream onto each cake. Cut each top in half so you have two 'wings' and arrange on top of each cake. Just before you want to eat them, sieve some icing sugar over the top: if you do it too soon the **icing sugar** will eventually sink into the cake.

Lemon Buttercream

50g (2oz) butter, softened
110g (4oz) icing sugar
1–2 tablespoons lemon juice

Beat the softened butter until creamy in a largish bowl. Sieve in the icing sugar, a little at a time. Finally, stir in the lemon juice to loosen it slightly.

Little Chocolate Cakes

These are beautifully chocolately and perfect for children's parties.

MAKES ABOUT 18 CAKES

175g (6oz) butter, softened
175g (6oz) unrefined caster sugar

150g (5oz) very fresh self-raising flour
or
150g (5oz) plain flour
1 level teaspoon bicarbonate of soda
2 level teaspoons cream of tartar

3 eggs
25g (1oz) good quality cocoa powder (not drinking chocolate)
2 tablespoons milk

You will need a 12-cup muffin tin plus paper cases.

1. Preheat the oven to 180°C (fan oven) or equivalent.

2. Whiz the butter and sugar together in a food processor until combined and fluffy. Sieve some of the flour in a layer over the mixture and then add the eggs. Sieve in the rest of the flour, the cream of tartar and bicarbonate of soda and the cocoa. Whiz again. Add the milk and whiz until smooth and glossy. You may need to remove the lid a couple of times and scrape the mixture down from the sides with a flexible spatula.

3. Arrange the paper cases in the muffin tin and spoon 2 fairly generous teaspoons of mixture into each case. Bake for around 15 minutes or until domed and risen and springy to the touch. A skewer or wooden cocktail stick should come out clean when inserted. Remove from the tin with a small palette knife and leave to cool on a wire rack. Bake the remaining part batch. They can be decorated with **Chocolate Glacé Icing**, page 62.

Chocolate Glacé Icing

200g (7oz) icing sugar
25g (1oz) cocoa powder
4 tablespoons milk
2 teaspoons glycerine

1. Sieve about a quarter of the icing sugar and cocoa powder into a large bowl and stir in the milk and glycerine. Sieve the rest of the icing sugar and cocoa in a bit at a time until it is all incorporated. Beat with a wooden spoon until glossy. Spoon over the cooled cakes. You can either spread the icing over the whole top of the cake or spoon a little circle of icing into the middle of each cake.

Chocolate Butterfly Cakes

The mixture on page 60 also makes great butterfly cakes. You can make them with either **Chocolate Buttercream**, page 63, or **Lemon and Vanilla Buttercream**. It's quite nice if you are having a bit of a party to make half with chocolate and half with vanilla and arrange them on the same plate. If you need to soften the butter quickly, try putting it in the microwave on high for 10–20 seconds.

Chocolate Buttercream

75g (3oz) butter, softened
25g (1oz) good quality cocoa powder
150g (5oz) icing sugar
A little milk to mix

1. Combine the cocoa and icing sugar and sieve into the softened butter a little at a time, mixing it all together with a wooden spoon. Finally, loosen the mixture slightly with the milk and beat until smooth and glossy.

2. Once the cakes are cool, slice the tops off and put to one side. Spoon a little dollop of buttercream onto each cake. Cut each top in half so you have two 'wings' and arrange on top of each cake. Just before you want to eat them, sieve some icing sugar over the top: if you do it too soon the icing sugar will eventually sink into the cake.

Lemon and Vanilla Buttercream Icing

50g (2oz) butter, softened
110g (4oz) icing sugar
Few drops of vanilla extract or $^1/_2$ teaspoon of vanilla bean paste
Squeeze of lemon juice

1. Cream the butter in a bowl large enough to give you room to manoeuvre. Use a wooden spoon. Gradually add the icing sugar, passing it through a sieve. When the icing sugar is all combined, add the vanilla and stir in a squeeze of lemon juice, just enough to loosen the mixture slightly.

Cup Cakes

A cup cake is very like a fairy cake but much more glamorous and opulent. Cup cakes tend to be topped with a swirl of buttercream rather than glacé icing and you can really enjoy yourself decorating them and making them look fabulous. Don't hold back: they are meant to look a bit extravagant!

You can adapt the basic recipe oposite to make five more different flavours. You might like to make a mixed batch: home-baked cup cakes are always popular as gifts. You can swap the buttercream icings round if you like: chocolate cup cake with coffee icing or raspberry cup cake with lemon and vanilla icing, for example. Cup cakes are also perfect for celebrations, arranged on a stand for weddings and parties or lavishly and lovingly decorated for Valentine's Day.

These cup cakes are made in paper muffin cases in a muffin tin, so they are a little larger than fairy cakes.

Original Cup Cakes

These are lovely and light.

MAKES 12 CAKES

175g (6oz) butter, softened
175g (6oz) unrefined caster sugar
175g (6oz) plain flour
3 eggs, beaten
1 level teaspoon bicarbonate of soda
2 level teaspoons cream of tartar
2 tablespoons milk

You will need a 12-cup muffin tin plus paper muffin cases.

1. Preheat the oven to 160°C (fan oven) or equivalent.

2. Whiz the butter and sugar together in a food processor until combined and fluffy. Sieve in some of the flour and add the eggs. Sieve in the rest of the flour, the bicarbonate of soda and cream of tartar. Whiz again. Add the milk and whiz until smooth and glossy. You may need to scrape the mixture down from the sides a couple of times with a flexible spatula.

3. Arrange the paper cases in the muffin tin and, using a dessertspoon, divide the mixture equally between the cases.

4. Bake for around 18 minutes or until risen and pale golden and springy to the touch. A skewer or wooden cocktail stick should come out clean when inserted.

5. Allow to rest for a few minutes and then remove from the tin and cool on a wire rack.

Lemon Buttercream

50g (2oz) butter, softened
110g (4oz) icing sugar
1–2 tablespoons lemon juice

Beat the butter in a largish bowl until creamy. Sieve in the icing sugar, a little at a time. Finally, stir in the lemon juice to loosen it slightly.

Assembling the cup cakes

Swirl the buttercream over the top of each cake so that it either completely covers the top or arrange it in a large circle so that there is a narrow rim of cake showing around the edge. You can then go to town with the decorations of your choice.

Vanilla Cup Cakes

Follow the **Original Cup Cakes** recipe on page 65 but add **1 teaspoon of vanilla extract or vanilla bean paste** to the beaten eggs before you add them to the cake mixture. Ice with the lemon and vanilla buttercream, below.

Lemon and Vanilla Buttercream

Add $^1/_2$ teaspoon **vanilla extract** or **vanilla bean paste** to the **Lemon Buttercream** icing, above.

A single chocolate chip (milk or white chocolate) or a sprinkling of crushed nuts make an attractive decoration.

Lemon Cup Cakes

Follow the **Original Cup Cakes** recipe on page 65 but add the **finely grated zest of** $^1/_2$ **a lemon** to the cake mixture. Ice with the **Lemon Buttercream**, page 66.

A *tiny* amount of *very* finely grated lemon zest or some pale and pretty cake decorations look attractive on top.

Raspberry Cup Cakes

These have the most delicious, understated and elusive raspberry flavour and are golden brown in colour. The pale peachy-pink buttercream looks very glamorous and wedding-like.

Use only **110g (4oz) of sugar** in the **Original Cup Cakes** mixture and also add **2 rounded tablespoons of seedless raspberry jam**. Cream the jam with the sugar and softened butter in the usual way.

The raspberry version bakes a little more quickly: test after 15 minutes, but as always, be aware that oven performance can vary tremendously.

Ice with **Raspberry Buttercream**, below.

Raspberry Buttercream

Add **1–2 gently rounded teaspoons of seedless raspberry jam** to the **Lemon Buttercream**, page 66.

If you are making these for a wedding or wedding anniversary, gold or silver cake decorations look particularly stylish.

Coffee Cup Cakes

Add **2 teaspoons of instant espresso coffee powder** to the flour for the **Original Cup Cakes** mixture on page 65. Ice with **Coffee Buttercream**, below.

If you can, make the **Coffee Buttercream** a few hours ahead of time, and keep it cool and covered (preferably not in the fridge as it will set too hard). This gives the coffee flavour a chance to mellow and develop.

Coffee Buttercream

75g (3oz) butter, softened
175g (6oz) icing sugar
2 teaspoons instant espresso coffee powder
1–2 tablespoons water, just off the boil

Dissolve the coffee powder in the hot water and set aside. Sieve the icing sugar into the softened butter a little at a time, mixing it all together with a wooded spoon. Finally, stir in the dissolved coffee and beat until smooth and glossy.

You may like to sprinkle the top of the cakes with cocoa, drinking chocolate powder or even cinnamon to give a kind of cappuccino effect. Alternatively, decorate with grated chocolate, chocolate chips, chocolate bean sweets or chocolate-coated coffee beans. Walnut or pecan halves are also good, giving a traditional 'coffee cake' look to the cup cakes.

Chocolate Cup Cakes

Use 150g (5oz) of flour in the **Original Cup Cakes** mixture on page 65 with 25g (1oz) of good quality cocoa powder (not drinking chocolate) and add **1 teaspoon of vanilla extract**. Ice with **Chocolate Buttercream**, below.

Chocolate Buttercream

25g (1oz) good quality cocoa powder
75g (3oz) icing sugar
50g (2oz) butter, softened
¼ teaspoon vanilla extract
1–2 tablespoons milk

Sieve the combined cocoa and icing sugar into the softened butter a little at a time, mixing it all together with a wooden spoon. Stir in the vanilla. Finally, loosen the mixture slightly with the milk and beat until smooth and glossy.

Decorate with grated chocolate, chocolate chips or chocolate bean sweets, crushed nuts or anything else you fancy.

Plain and Simple Sponge Cake

This is the classic Victoria Sandwich. Apparently, Queen Victoria
herself was very fond of this type of sponge cake 'sandwiched'
simply with jam.

175g (6oz) butter, softened
175g (6oz) unrefined caster sugar
175g (6oz) plain flour
2 level teaspoons cream of tartar
1 level teaspoon bicarbonate of soda
3 eggs
2 tablespoons milk
Good quality jam such as seedless raspberry or bramble jelly (strawberry
can be a bit sweet to fill a sweet sponge cake)
Icing sugar, to finish

You will need 2 greased 18cm (7in) loose-bottomed sandwich tins.

1. Preheat the oven to 180°C (fan oven) or equivalent, see opposite.

2. Whiz the butter and sugar together in a food processor until light
and fluffy. Sieve the flour in carefully with the cream of tartar and
bicarbonate of soda, and add the eggs. Whiz again. Add the milk and
whiz until very smooth and glossy and everything is well mixed. You
may need to scrape the mixture down from the sides a couple of
times with a flexible spatula.

3. You should now have a dropping consistency. That is to say, the
mixture isn't so thick that it won't drop easily off a spoon, but it isn't
runny either.

4. Pour into the prepared cake tins using a flexible spatula to help all
the mixture out.

5. Bake in the middle of the oven for 18–20 minutes until the cakes are risen and golden and a skewer inserted comes out clean.

6. Allow the cakes to rest for a few moments and then carefully loosen the edges with a small palette knife: they should be starting to contract away from the sides of their own accord.

7. If the tins are still too hot to handle, stand the cakes, one at a time, on a jar or something similar. Using both hands, protected with an oven glove or tea towel, pull the side of the tin down so the cake is left, still on its base, on top of the jar. Move it closer to your cooling rack and loosen from the base using a large palette knife. Transfer gently (you may need a fish slice as well as the palette knife at this stage) onto the cooling rack. Repeat with the other cake.

8. Try not to flip the cake over straight out of the tin onto the cooling rack. This manoeuvre will leave you with deep lines or squares indented across the top of your cake, which doesn't look very professional: should you ever wish to enter your sponge cake into a baking competition, you would be marked down for this!

9. Once the cakes are cool, spread one with jam; position the other on top, and sieve icing sugar over it.

Sponge cake temperatures

Suggested temperatures for baking sponge cakes of this type can vary from 160°C to 190°C (fan oven). If your oven is a fairly steady average performer, set it to 180°C. If you have a very fierce oven, 160°C may be preferable. If the finished sponge comes out of the oven flat and hard, it is likely the temperature was too high and the top cooked before the centre could rise. If the sponge comes out of the oven heavy and not completely cooked, it is likely that the temperature was too low or it wasn't cooked for long enough. It may be that you will have to have a couple of attempts before you get it right, but keep notes and persevere: you will get there in the end!

Light Lemon Sponge

Add the **very finely grated zest of half a lemon** to the **Plain and Simple Sponge Cake** recipe, page 70.

Once the cake has cooled, fill with **Lemon Buttercream** as on page 66 and sieve some **icing sugar** over the top.

Extra Special Lemon Sponge

Make the **Light Lemon Sponge** as above. Sandwich together with lemon curd. Ice the top with **Glacé Icing**, page 73.

Sponge Cake with Jam and Buttercream

Again, make a perfectly **Simple Sponge Cake**, as page 70. Spread the lower half with **jam** and then carefully spread **Lemon Buttercream**, on page 66, over the top of the jam, using a small palette knife. Put the top cake on and sieve **icing sugar** over it.

Old-fashioned Birthday Cake

This is a really simple, old fashioned, cake-shaped birthday cake.

Make the **Plain and Simple Sponge Cake** as page 70. Sandwich with jam and coat the top with the glacé icing below.

Glacé Icing

175g (6oz) icing sugar
3 tablespoons lemon juice
2 teaspoons glycerine

1. Sieve the icing sugar into a large bowl and stir in the lemon juice and glycerine. Beat with a wooden spoon until smooth and glossy.

2. Spoon the icing carefully over the cake: aim to keep it all on top of the cake but if a little drizzles down the sides don't worry, it will just look more traditional, like a cake in a child's picture book.

3. For Pink Icing, see the **Fairy Cakes** section.

Chocolate Cake

This is a lovely, easy-to-make chocolate cake for any occasion and just perfect for a birthday tea.

175g (6oz) butter, softened
175g (6oz) unrefined caster sugar
150g (5oz) plain flour
3 eggs
1 level teaspoon bicarbonate of soda
2 level teaspoons cream of tartar
25g (1oz) good quality cocoa powder (not drinking chocolate)
2 tablespoons milk

You will need 2 greased 18cm (7in) loose-bottomed sandwich tins.

1. Preheat the oven to 180°C (fan oven) or equivalent.

2. Whiz the butter and sugar together in a food processor until combined and fluffy. Sieve some of the flour in a layer over the mixture and then add the eggs. Sieve in the rest of the flour, bicarbonate of soda, cream of tartar and cocoa. Whiz again. Add the milk and whiz until smooth and glossy.

3. You may need to remove the lid a couple of times and scrape the mixture down from the sides with a flexible spatula.

4. Turn into the greased sandwich tins and bake for 18–20 minutes or until nicely risen and firm but springy to the touch. A wooden cocktail stick inserted into the cake should come out clean.

5. Allow the cakes to rest for a few moments and then carefully loosen the edges with a small palette knife: they should be starting to contract away from the sides of their own accord.

6. If the tins are too hot to handle, stand the cakes, one at a time, on a jar or something similar. Using both hands, pull the side of the tin down so the cake is left, still on its base, on top of the jar. Move it closer to your cooling rack and loosen from the base using a large palette knife. Transfer gently (you may need a fish slice as well as the palette knife at this stage) onto the cooling rack. Repeat with the other cake.

7. See **Little Chocolate Cakes** and **Chocolate Butterfly Cakes**, in the previous section for **Chocolate Buttercream** and **Chocolate Glacé Icing**.

8. Spread some of the buttercream carefully onto one of the sponges with a small palette knife. Put the second sponge on top and spread the rest of the buttercream over it. You might like to grate some chocolate over the top to decorate.

9. Alternatively, make a half quantity of buttercream and ice the top with chocolate glacé icing instead.

Dorset Apple Cake

This is a lovely cake for any time of year but especially in the autumn when there are so many apples around. It's really easy to make and is delicious warm or cold. It goes very well indeed with a dollop of clotted cream.

225g (8oz) plain flour
1¹/2 level teaspoons baking powder
110g (4oz) butter
110g (4oz) unrefined granulated sugar, plus a little more for the top
75g (3oz) currants or raisins
225g (8oz) peeled and cored apples, finely chopped (cooking, eating or a mixture of both)
2 eggs, beaten

You will need a greased, loose-bottomed 20cm (8in) cake tin.

1. Preheat the oven to 160°C (fan oven) or equivalent.

2. Sieve the flour and baking powder into a bowl and rub in the butter. Stir in the sugar, dried fruit and apple. Mix in the eggs. Turn into the prepared tin and smooth the top with the back of a metal spoon: a wet spoon makes it easier. Sprinkle some more sugar over the top. Cover loosely with greaseproof paper, tucking it underneath the tin to secure, and bake the cake for approximately 40–45 minutes, until golden on top.

3. Leave in the tin for a few moments, then remove and cool on a wire rack. Store in an airtight tin.

Apple and Sultana Spice Cake

You will notice that this is a kind of cross between the two previous cakes. It is packed full of goodness with an extra touch of spice, all topped off with a little sprinkling of cinnamon sugar. Again, this cake goes beautifully with clotted cream. A slice is also just the thing to keep you going if you've missed breakfast.

110g (4oz) plain flour
1/2 teaspoon baking powder
2 teaspoons cinnamon
1 teaspoon mixed spice
110g (4oz) wholemeal flour
110g (4oz) butter
110g (4oz) unrefined granulated sugar
110g (4oz) sultanas
3 eggs
275g (10oz) peeled and cored apples
(cooking, eating or a mixture of both)

Plus, approximately another 1/2 teaspoon of cinnamon and 1 teaspoon unrefined granulated sugar for the top

You will need a greased, loose-bottomed 20cm (8in) cake tin.

1. Preheat the oven to 160°C (fan oven) or equivalent.

2. Sieve the plain flour into a bowl with the baking powder and spices. Stir in the wholemeal flour. Cut the butter into small dice and rub into the flour mixture and stir in the sugar and sultanas. Blend in the eggs with a wooden spoon so that all the dry ingredients are moist and coated with egg: it will still look quite rough and crumbly.

3. Slice the apples in half and place flat side down on a board. Cut one of the apples into bite-sized chunks and chop the rest fairly finely. Stir into the cake mixture.

4. Smooth the top of the cake with the back of a metal spoon: wet the spoon to make it easier. Stir the extra sugar and cinnamon together in a small bowl and sprinkle lightly over the top. Cover loosely with greaseproof paper, tucking it underneath the tin to secure and bake in a preheated oven for 40–45 minutes, depending on the ferocity of your oven, until springy to the touch and a skewer inserted comes out clean.

5. Leave in the tin for a few moments, then remove and cool on a wire rack. Store in an airtight tin. Eat warm or cold.

Banana Cake

The bananas for this recipe need to be just over-ripe: the skins should be a bit speckled and the banana should look slightly mealy but still be white. Don't be tempted to add any more banana 'just to use it up' as too much banana will make the cake solid and heavy.

110g (4oz) butter, softened
110g (4oz) soft light brown sugar
110g (4oz) wholemeal flour
50g (2oz) plain flour
50g (2oz) ground almonds
2 level teaspoons cream of tartar
1 level teaspoon bicarbonate of soda
2 fresh eggs
150–175g (5–6oz) ripe bananas (peeled weight), mashed to a purée but not liquidy

You will need a greased 18cm (7in) loose-bottomed cake tin.

1. Preheat the oven to 160°C (fan oven) or equivalent.

2. Whiz the butter and sugar together in a food processor. Add the flours, ground almonds, cream of tartar, bicarbonate of soda and eggs and whiz until combined. Finally, add the banana and whiz that in too.

3. Spoon into the prepared tin, cover loosely with greaseproof paper and bake for about 40–45 minutes, or until a skewer inserted into the cake comes out clean.

4. Loosen the sides and bottom with a palette knife, remove from the tin and cool on a wire rack.

Banana Buns and Little Loaves

You might prefer to make banana buns instead: individual cakes are always popular. All you do is make the mixture as page 79 but spoon it into a greased 12-cup muffin tin or 12 greased mini-loaf tins instead. (There is no need to cover with greaseproof paper.) Bake at the same temperature as for the cake for 20 minutes, or until they are springy to the touch and a skewer comes out clean.

Over-ripe banana alert!
This is a useful recipe if you have a couple of bananas that are well past their best: as long as they are pale brown rather than actually black inside, you can still use them, even if the skins are more brown than yellow.

Carrot Cake

Carrot cake tastes quite indulgent whilst also being packed full of good and healthy ingredients! The cinnamon in this recipe gives a hint of warmth and depth, the orange zest a lovely freshness and the orange buttercream icing (page 82) a touch of luxury.

110g (4oz) butter, softened
110g (4oz) soft brown sugar
110g (4oz) wholemeal flour
50g (2oz) plain flour
50g (2oz) ground almonds
2 level teaspoons baking powder
1 teaspoon ground cinnamon
2 eggs
150g (5oz) grated carrot (grated weight)
Finely grated zest of 1 orange

You will need a greased 18cm (7in) loose-bottomed cake tin.

1. Preheat the oven to 160°C (fan oven) or equivalent.

2. Whiz the butter and sugar together in a food processor. Add the flours, ground almonds, baking powder, cinnamon and eggs and whiz until combined. Finally, add the grated carrot and orange zest and whiz again.

3. Spoon into the prepared tin, cover loosely with greaseproof paper and bake for about 40–45 minutes, or until a skewer inserted into the cake comes out clean.

4. Loosen the sides and bottom with a palette knife, remove from tin and cool on a wire rack.

Carrot Buns and Little Loaves

This recipe also makes brilliant buns. Make the recipe as above but spoon into a greased 12-cup muffin tin or 12 greased mini-loaf tins instead. There is no need to cover. Bake at the same temperature for 20 minutes or until a skewer comes out clean.

Optional icing
Again, both the cake and buns are lovely on their own, but carrot cake is wonderful iced. **Orange Buttercream** (page 82) makes a delicious change from the usual cream cheese frosting.

Orange Buttercream Icing

Cream the butter in a bowl large enough to give you room to manoeuvre. Use a wooden spoon. Gradually add the icing sugar, passing it through a sieve. When the icing sugar is all combined, stir in the orange juice, just enough to loosen the mixture slightly.

Spread onto the top of the cake or buns.

Lemon Drizzle Cake

This is a classic tea-time Lemon Drizzle Cake: not too sweet, and not too sharp, moist and light. This recipe gives you the option to make either a loaf-shaped cake or a round one.

For the cake
110g (4oz) butter, softened
110g (4oz) unrefined caster sugar
175g (6oz) plain flour
2 eggs, beaten
1 level teaspoon bicarbonate of soda
2 level teaspoons of cream of tartar
Grated zest of 1 lemon
2 tablespoons warm water

For the drizzle
Juice of 2 lemons
2 level tablespoons unrefined caster sugar

You will need a greased 450g (1lb) loaf tin (in good condition, preferably anodised) or an 18cm (7in) round, loose-bottomed cake tin.

1. Preheat the oven to 160°C (fan oven) or equivalent.

2. Whiz the butter and sugar together until combined and fluffy. Carefully sieve in some of the flour to cover the surface of the butter and sugar and add the eggs. Add the rest of the flour, bicarbonate of soda, cream of tartar, lemon zest and warm water. Whiz until everything is smooth and glossy. You may need to stop the machine a couple of times and scrape the mixture down from the sides.

3. Pour into the prepared tin and cover loosely with greaseproof paper, tucking it under the tin to secure. You need to have the tension of the paper just right so that it protects the cake from drying out without dipping down onto the surface and sticking to it.

4. Bake for 45–50 minutes for the loaf cake and 40–45 for the round cake, until risen and golden and a skewer inserted comes out clean.

5. Whilst the cake is baking, heat the lemon juice and sugar together in a small heavy-bottomed saucepan, stirring frequently until the sugar has dissolved. Put aside to cool.

6. When the cake is ready, leave it in its tin and prick the surface lightly: if you have a fairly thick needle this won't make such noticeable holes as a cocktail stick or fork. Spoon the drizzle evenly all over the top. If you have one of those Perspex gravy separators with a thin, round spout, this would be ideal for pouring the drizzle over with. Alternatively, spoon it over.

7. Keep the cake in the tin until it is completely cold and the drizzle has soaked in. Transfer to an airtight tin.

Traditional Rock Buns with Currants and Lemon

These buns are absolutely delicious and so easy to make.
Incidentally, they are meant to look a bit like little rocks: not
actually have a rock-like texture!

MAKES 12 BUNS

225g (8oz) plain flour

2 level teaspoons baking powder
or
2 level teaspoons cream of tartar
1 level teaspoon bicarbonate of soda

110g (4oz) butter
110g (4oz) unrefined caster sugar
110g (4oz) currants
Finely grated zest of 1 lemon
1 egg
2 tablespoons milk

You will need a greased baking tray.

1. Preheat the oven to 180°C (fan oven) or equivalent.

2. Zest the lemon in very quick, short up-and-down movements as
nobody wants to end up with long strands of peel dangling from
their mouths!

3. Sieve the flour and raising agents and rub in the butter. Stir in the sugar and currants, the egg and milk. It will look a bit rough and dry to start with but you will soon have a fairly stiff, but pliable, dough.

4. Divide the dough into 12 and roll into balls: you may like to wet your hands first if it seems a bit sticky. Spread them out on the prepared baking tray. Bake for about 12 minutes until they are golden on top and a skewer inserted comes out clean.

5. Don't overcook them unless you are intentionally aiming for an authentic rock-like consistency! They should be slightly crisp on the outside and light and crumbly on the inside.

6. Cool on a wire rack and store in an airtight tin when cold. Eat within a couple of days.

Cranberry and Orange Rock Buns

These are an extremely yummy version of the pevious recipe. Instead of currants, use the same amount of dried cranberries, and instead of finely grated lemon zest, use finely grated orange zest. As with the previous recipe, zest the orange in a quick up and down movement so that you get very short, broken shreds: nobody wants to cope with great long strands in their bun!

Madeira Cake

The lemon zest gives the cake a lovely freshness, but it is perfectly nice without. This recipe contains less sugar than is often used – more sugar gives a beautiful fine texture – but the texture of this version is still light and delicate.

110g (4oz) butter, softened
110g (4oz) unrefined caster sugar
175g (6oz) plain flour
2 eggs
1 level teaspoon bicarbonate of soda
2 level teaspoons cream of tartar
Grated zest of 1 lemon (optional)
2 tablespoons warm water

You will need a greased 450g (1lb) loaf tin or 18cm (7in) round, loose-bottomed cake tin.

1. Preheat the oven to 160°C (fan oven) or equivalent.

2. Whiz the butter and sugar together until combined and fluffy. Carefully sieve in some of the flour and add the eggs. Then add the rest of the flour, bicarbonate of soda, cream of tartar and the lemon zest, if using. Whiz briefly, and add the warm water. Whiz until everything is mixed together but not over mixed. You may need to stop the machine a couple of times and scrape the mixture down from the sides.

3. Pour into the prepared tin and cover loosely with greaseproof paper, tucking it under the tin to secure. You need to have the tension of the paper just right so that it protects the cake from drying out without dipping down onto the surface and sticking to it.

4. Bake for 45–50 minutes for the loaf cake and 40–45 for the round cake, until risen and golden and a skewer inserted comes out clean.

5. Leave in the tin for a while to settle and contract away from the sides.

Seed Cake

The caraway seeds give the cake the most beautiful flavour. Stir them in at the end, as directed, to keep them whole and undamaged. Options are given for both a round and a loaf-shaped cake.

110g (4oz) butter, softened
110g (4oz) unrefined caster sugar
175g (6oz) plain flour
2 eggs
1 level teaspoon bicarbonate of soda
2 level teaspoons cream of tartar
2 tablespoons warm water
2 teaspoons caraway seeds

You will need a greased 450g (1lb) loaf tin or 18cm (7in) round, loose-bottomed cake tin.

1. Preheat the oven to 160°C (fan oven) or equivalent.

2. Whiz the butter and sugar together until combined and fluffy. Carefully sieve in some of the flour and add the eggs. Then add the rest of the flour, the bicarbonate of soda and cream of tartar. Whiz briefly and add the warm water. Whiz until everything is mixed together but not over mixed. You may need to stop the machine a couple of times and scrape the mixture down from the sides.

3. Remove the blade from the machine and stir in the caraway seeds.

4. Pour into the prepared tin and cover loosely with greaseproof paper, tucking it under the tin to secure. You need to have the tension of the paper just right so that it protects the cake from drying out without dipping down onto the surface and sticking to it.

5. Bake for 45–50 minutes for the loaf cake and 40–45 for the round cake, until risen and golden and a skewer inserted comes out clean.

6. Leave in the tin for a while to settle and contract away from the sides – particularly if you are using a loaf tin – then transfer to a wire rack until completely cold. Once cold, store in an airtight tin.

Cherry Cake

If you are fond of glacé cherries, you can adapt this mixture for a classic cherry cake recipe. If the glacé cherries look a bit syrupy, wash them gently and dry them with a clean cloth before using. If you don't, they can sink and you'll have a kind of cherry layer cake with sunken cherries as the bottom layer! Don't forget to toss them in flour as well, as this also helps to keep them afloat.

110g (4oz) butter, softened
110g (4oz) unrefined caster sugar
175g (6oz) plain flour
2 eggs
1 level teaspoon bicarbonate of soda
2 level teaspoons cream of tartar
2 tablespoons warm water
110g (4oz) glacé cherries, halved or quartered, or dried sour cherries

You will need a greased 450g (1lb) loaf tin or 18cm (7in) round, loose-bottomed cake tin.

1. Preheat the oven to 160°C (fan oven) or equivalent.

2. Take about a tablespoon of flour from the amount you have measured out and toss the glacé cherries in it. Set aside until the end when you stir them in.

3. Whiz the butter and sugar together until combined and fluffy. Carefully sieve in some of the flour and add the eggs. Add the rest of the flour, the bicarbonate of soda and cream of tartar. Whiz briefly and add the warm water. Whiz until everything is mixed together but not over mixed. You may need to stop the machine a couple of times and scrape the mixture down from the sides.

4. Remove the blade from the machine and stir in the floured glacé cherries or dried sour cherries.

5. Pour into the prepared tin and cover loosely with greaseproof paper, tucking it under the tin to secure. You need to have the tension of the paper just right so that it protects the cake from drying out without dipping down onto the surface and sticking to it.

6. Bake for 45–50 minutes for the loaf cake and 40–45 for the round cake, until risen and golden and a skewer inserted comes out clean.

7. Leave in the tin for a while to settle and contract away from the sides – particularly if you are using a loaf tin – then transfer to a wire rack until completely cold. Once cold, store in an airtight tin.

Coconut Cake

You can also adapt the same mixture again to make a lovely, moist coconut cake.

110g (4oz) butter, softened
110g (4oz) unrefined caster sugar
110g (4oz) plain flour
2 eggs
1 level teaspoon bicarbonate of soda
2 level teaspoons cream of tartar
2 tablespoons warm water
50g (2oz) desiccated coconut

You will need a greased 450g (1lb) loaf tin or 18cm (7in) round, loose-bottomed cake tin.

1. Preheat the oven to 160°C (fan oven) or equivalent.

2. Whiz the butter and sugar together until combined and fluffy. Carefully sieve in some of the flour and add the eggs. Add the rest of the flour, the bicarbonate of soda and cream of tartar. Whiz briefly and add the warm water. Whiz until everything is mixed together but not over mixed. You may need to stop the machine a couple of times and scrape the mixture down from the sides.

3. Finally, add the coconut and whiz briefly to mix it all in evenly.

4. Pour into the prepared tin and cover loosely with greaseproof paper, tucking it under the tin to secure. You need to have the tension of the paper just right so that it protects the cake from drying out without dipping down onto the surface and sticking to it.

5. Bake for approximately 40–45 minutes until risen and golden and a skewer inserted comes out clean.

6. Leave in the tin for a while to settle and contract away from the sides – particularly if you are using a loaf tin.

7. Even if you are using a loaf tin, provided you have a decent one in good shape (an anodised one is good) and have greased it sufficiently, you shouldn't need to line it. Once the cake has cooled and is starting to pull away from the sides, press gently on the edge of the cake, all the way round the sides, to pull it away further. You may need the very gentlest of help with a small palette knife as well. Shake the tin sideways briskly a couple of times and you should then be able to turn it out.

8. Transfer to a wire rack until completely cold. Once cold, store in an airtight tin.

Coconut Buns

You can adapt any of the recipes in this section to make buns instead. The coconut version is especially delicious in bun form and very popular with children.

Make the mixture as for the **Coconut Cake** recipe on page 92 and grease a 12-cup muffin tin. Using a dessertspoon, divide the mixture equally between the 12 cups. Bake at 160°C as before, for approximately 12–15 minutes until risen and golden and a skewer inserted comes out clean.

Leave to settle in the tin for a few minutes – they are very fragile at this stage. Then, lever them out very gently, using a small palette knife and transfer to a wire rack to finish cooling. Once completely cold, store in an airtight container.

Coconut and Raspberry Buns

The Coconut Buns are also fabulous split and spread with raspberry jam. Who would have thought the fruit of the exotic coconut palm, swaying on tropical beaches, and the cool climate raspberry could strike up such a winning partnership? Despite the geographical gulf between them, theirs is a marriage made in heaven.

Slice each bun in half horizontally and sandwich together with raspberry jam (use seedless if you don't like the pips). If it is a special occasion, sieve a little icing sugar over the top of each bun just before serving: use a tea strainer and stir the icing sugar through with a teaspoon. These are possibly even more popular with children than the plain coconut buns.

Cherry and Coconut Cake

Cherries and coconut are another classic combination. If you are fond of cherries there is nothing to stop you adding some to your coconut cake. Proceed as before but halve or quarter 50g (2oz) of glacé cherries and toss them in a little of the flour you have measured out. Put aside and, once the cake is mixed, remove the processor blade and gently stir in the floured cherries. Continue as before.

Apple Crumble Cake

This scrumptious cake is like eating two favourites at the same time: apple crumble and apple cake! It tastes great served either cold as a cake or warm from the oven with clotted cream as a pudding. It has a denser, moister texture when warm; when cold, the texture is much finer.

For the cake
110g (4oz) butter, softened
110g (4oz) unrefined caster sugar
50g (2oz) ground almonds
175g (6oz) plain flour
2 eggs
1 level teaspoon bicarbonate of soda
2 level teaspoons cream of tartar
4 tablespoons milk

For the fruit topping
A couple of dessert apples weighing approximately 225g (8oz) (peeled and cored weight), Cox's are perfect

For the crumble topping
20g (¾oz) butter
50g (2oz) plain flour
¼ teaspoon baking powder
20g (¾oz) unrefined granulated sugar

You will need a greased 18cm (7in) loose-bottomed cake tin.

1. Preheat the oven to 160°C (fan oven) or equivalent.

2. Whiz the butter and sugar together thoroughly in the food processor until light and fluffy. Add the ground almonds and whiz to combine. Sieve half of the flour over the top and add the eggs. Sieve the rest of

the flour, bicarbonate of soda and cream of tartar over the top and whiz. Add the milk and whiz until everything is fully mixed and smooth. Stop the processor a couple of times and scrape the mixture down from the sides with a flexible spatula.

3. Cut the peeled and cored apples in half and lay them cut side down on a board. Cut into slices of about half a centimetre.

4. Make the crumble topping by rubbing the butter, flour and baking powder together and stir in the sugar.

5. Pour the cake mixture into the prepared tin and layer the apple slices over the surface. Scatter the crumble evenly over the top.

6. Cover the tin loosely with greaseproof paper, tucking it underneath to secure. Bake for about 1¾ hours until the top is golden and a skewer inserted comes out clean (you may like to remove the greaseproof paper for the last 15 minutes or so). Transfer to a wire rack and store in an airtight container when completely cold.

✓ **Helpful note**
Don't try to make a crumble mix with the bowl on the worktop – it's too high and you'll feel awkward. Put the bowl on a table instead, it's much more comfortable.

Plum Crumble Cake

Make this in exactly the same way as the **Apple Crumble Cake**, page 96, but instead of apple, use the amount of stoned plums specified below, arranging the plum halves over the top of the cake cut-side down.

Approximately 225g (8oz) or a fraction more plums, Victoria, Marjorie's Seedling, or similar. This will equate to about **7 or 8 plums**.

Cherry and Almond Cake

This cake has the most delicious flavour: it's not over-sweet as the dried cherries used are slightly tart. Flaked almonds on top of a cake always make it look instantly professional.

110g (4oz) butter, softened
110g (4oz) unrefined caster sugar
175g (6oz) plain flour
2 fresh eggs
1 level teaspoon bicarbonate of soda
2 level teaspoons cream of tartar
4 tablespoons milk
50g (2oz) ground almonds
100–110g (3^1/2–4oz) dried cherries (sometimes called dried
sour cherries)
Approximately 25g (1oz) flaked almonds, to decorate

You will need a greased 18cm (7in) loose-bottomed cake tin.

1. Preheat the oven to 160°C (fan oven) or equivalent.

2. Separate the cherries, and cut any that look a bit big in half with kitchen scissors. Take about a tablespoon of flour from the measured amount and toss the cherries in it: although they are dried, they are still moist enough to have a tendency to sink. Set aside until needed.

3. Whiz the butter and sugar together thoroughly in the food processor until light and fluffy. Sieve half of the flour over the top and add the eggs. Sieve the rest of the flour, bicarbonate of soda and cream of tartar over the top and whiz. Add the milk and ground almonds and whiz until everything is fully mixed and smooth. Stop the processor a couple of times and scrape the mixture down from the sides with a flexible spatula.

4. Remove the blade from the food processor and stir in the cherries, distributing them evenly throughout the mixture.

5. Ease the cake mixture into the prepared tin. Scatter the flaked almonds evenly over the top.

6. Cover the tin loosely with greaseproof paper, tucking it underneath to secure. Bake for about 45 minutes until the top is golden and a skewer inserted comes out clean.

7. Transfer to a wire rack and store in an airtight container when completely cold.

Rich, Dark, Moist Ginger Cake

This dark and sticky ginger cake is not for the faint-hearted.
Eat it fresh and fluffy on the first day after baking or leave it in an
airtight container for a couple of days to get denser and stickier.
Black treacle, incidentally, is good for you as it contains useful
amounts of iron.

110g (4oz) butter, cut into small pieces
75g (3oz) unrefined caster sugar
6 tablespoons black treacle
150ml (¼pt) water
225g (8oz) plain flour
1 level teaspoon bicarbonate of soda
2 level teaspoons cream of tartar
2 teaspoons mixed spice
3 teaspoons ground ginger
2 eggs

You will need a greased 450g (1lb) loaf tin, preferably lined.

1. Preheat the oven to 160°C (fan oven) or equivalent.

2. Put the butter, sugar, black treacle and water into a roomy pan.
Heat fairly gently until everything has melted and the sugar has
dissolved.

3. Put aside to cool a little – but don't let it go completely cold; it should still be warm or the cake won't rise as well.

4. Once cooler, but still slightly warm, sieve the flour, bicarbonate of soda, cream of tartar and spices over the mixture in several batches, stirring it in as you go, reserving a little of the flour to add with the eggs at the end.

5. Mix everything together thoroughly and finally add the eggs and the rest of the flour.

6. When everything is smooth and glossy, pour into the prepared tin: use a flexible spatula to scrape all the mixture out of the pan. Cover loosely with greaseproof paper and bake for approximately 45 minutes or until a skewer inserted comes out clean.

7. Leave in the tin for a while to cool slightly and contract away from the sides. Ease out of the tin: you may need to help it along gently with a small palette knife. Finish cooling on a wire rack.

8. Once completely cold, store in an airtight tin.

Useful note
Be sure to mix the flour in gradually and thoroughly: if you are a bit slap-dash you will end up with the odd little white blob of flour here and there in the finished cake.

Chocolate Brownie Buns

These have the taste of a brownie and the fluffiness of a bun with a gorgeously sticky top.

MAKES 12 BUNS

110g (4oz) butter, cut into small pieces
50g (2oz) soft dark brown sugar
6 tablespoons golden syrup
150ml (^{1}/4pt) water
200g (7oz) plain flour
1 level teaspoon bicarbonate of soda
2 level teaspoons cream of tartar
25g (1oz) cocoa powder (not drinking chocolate)
2 fresh eggs, beaten
1 teaspoon vanilla extract or vanilla bean paste

You will need a 12-cup bun tin and 12 muffin-size paper cases.

1. Preheat the oven to 160°C (fan oven) or equivalent.

2. Put the butter, sugar, golden syrup and water into a roomy pan. Heat fairly gently until everything has melted and the sugar has dissolved.

3. Put aside to cool a little – but don't let it go completely cold; it should still be warm or the buns won't rise as well.

4. Once cooler, but still slightly warm, sieve the flour, bicarbonate of soda, cream of tartar and cocoa over the mixture in several batches, stirring it in as you go, reserving a little of the flour to add with the eggs at the end.

5. Stir everything together thoroughly with a wooden spoon and finally add the vanilla to the beaten eggs and stir into the mixture with the rest of the flour. Keep mixing and, when everything is fully mixed and smooth and glossy, pour it all into a jug.

Note: If the mixture still appears to have the odd little lump in it, pour it all through a sieve for a completely smooth batter.

6. Pour into the paper cases in the bun tin. Fill each case to just over half way and try not to let any mixture spill over and down the sides of the cases. Scrape any mixture from the sides of the jug with a flexible spatula.

7. Bake for approximately 18 minutes or until a skewer inserted comes out clean.

8. Remove from the tin and finish cooling on a wire rack.

9. Once completely cold, store in an airtight tin.

Small Chocolate Brownie Buns

For a smaller bun, bake the previous recipe, still in a muffin tin, in fairy cake-size paper cases. Fill each case to just below the top and try to avoid spilling any down the sides.

Shorten the cooking time to approximately 16 minutes. You will need to bake a second part-batch.

Orange and Almond Buns

These buns are so delicious, and very versatile. Serve with a cup of tea or as part of a tea-time spread. Take them into the garden or on picnics. Alternatively, serve them as a pudding with some natural or Greek yoghurt. They are also wonderful for breakfast. They store well for up to a week, becoming slightly moister and stickier and more flavourful.

MAKES 12 BUNS

2 oranges, not too large: around about 150g (5oz) of pulped fruit is ideal
110g (4oz) butter), softened
110g (4oz) unrefined caster sugar
110g (4oz) plain flour
110g (4 oz) ground almonds
2 level teaspoons cream of tartar
1 level teaspoon bicarbonate of soda
2 eggs, beaten

You will need a greased 12-cup muffin tin.

1. Preheat the oven to 160°C (fan oven) or equivalent.

2. Take one of the oranges, remove the little green stalk part and put into a pan of cold water. Bring to the boil and simmer, partially covered, for about half to three quarters of an hour or until it is soft. Cool and cut into several pieces. Remove any pips and central pith, and any bits of membrane that will come away easily. Then put the rest into a food processor and whiz until it is an almost smooth, pale, orange-flecked purée.

3. Peel or grate all the zest from the second orange (a lemon zester works best) and add to the purée. Then add the butter and sugar and whiz until smooth. Finally, add the flour, ground almonds, cream of tartar, bicarbonate of soda and eggs and whiz until smooth and thoroughly mixed.

4. Spoon into the prepared tin. Bake for 12–15 minutes, or until pale golden on top, risen and firm to the touch, and a skewer inserted comes out clean.

5. Cool on a wire rack and eat warm or cold. The buns will keep in an airtight tin for up to a week.

Orange and Almond Cake

You will need a greased 18cm (7in) loose-bottomed cake tin and some greaseproof paper. Preheat the oven to 160°C (fan oven) or equivalent.

Make the cake mixture in exactly the same way as for the previous recipe, **Orange and Almond Buns**. Pour the mixture into the prepared tin and wrap the whole tin round with greaseproof paper. Bake for about 40–45 minutes, or until golden on top, firm to the touch, and a skewer inserted comes out clean.

Cool on a wire rack and eat warm or cold. The cake will keep in an airtight tin for up to a week.

Homemade Meringues

There is something very appealing about pale, buff-coloured meringues: they just look so deliciously homemade and appetising. Some people can be a bit sniffy about meringues that aren't sparkling white, but although it is very satisfying to pull off a pure white version, it *can* prompt comments like: 'You haven't *made* these, have you?', 'They're bought, aren't they?' In the end it's much less stressful all round to use unrefined caster sugar, plus it makes them look and taste absolutely lovely.

Despite what you might think, there is nothing difficult or scary about making a meringue – they are as easy as anything. What is more, they are inexpensive to make and only have two ingredients, they keep for up to six weeks in an airtight container *and* the finished meringues look impressive and taste delicious.

There are a few really simple pointers to bear in mind:

- The egg whites must be really fresh – not from ancient old eggs lurking at the back of the fridge.

- The bowl, whisk and spoons must be scrupulously clean and grease-free: make sure they have all been recently washed, preferably in the dishwasher, and that they are perfectly dry.

- Whisk the egg whites until you can do the classic thing of turning the bowl upside down without them falling out, but equally *don't over-beat them either*.

- It's important that the sugar is added *gradually*.

- Bake at a low temperature and line your baking sheet with lightly oiled greaseproof paper (or similar baking paper).

It's surprising how far egg white will go, so the following recipe is for just two egg whites, but you can increase the quantities proportionally. Some people fold the sugar in after the first spoonful, instead of whisking it, and you can do that if you like.

If you want your meringues to be explosively crisp and dry throughout, flatten and spread out the blobs of meringue on the baking tray. If you prefer them to have that dangerously moreish, delectable squidgy centre, then mound them up so they are higher and cover a smaller area.

MAKES ABOUT 12 INDIVIDUAL MERINGUES
(OR 1 LARGE ONE)

Very small amount of flavourless oil, such as rapeseed, for greasing
2 very fresh egg whites
110g (4oz) unrefined caster sugar

You will need an electric hand whisk or manual rotary whisk
and a large, lined baking sheet.

1. Preheat the oven to 100°C (fan oven) or equivalent.

2. Brush a very small amount of oil over the lined baking tray.

3. Whisk the egg white until stiff – or it might be more accurate to say lightly stiff, see above.

4. Add a tablespoonful of sugar, whisk it in and continue whisking in a spoonful at a time until all the sugar is incorporated – again, don't over-whisk it each time.

5. Using a dessertspoon, arrange single blobs of meringue on the prepared tray – space them out, not because they will spread, they won't, but you need to give each meringue a bit of room for the hot air to circulate.

6. Bake for an hour or until you can peel them off the paper easily. Leave them in the oven with the oven door slightly open until the oven has gone cold so they can finish drying out.

7. Once they are completely cold they will just lift off the tray. Store in an airtight container.

Note on piping meringue
If you prefer, you can pipe the meringue in whirls onto the baking tray, but you may feel it makes the meringues look a bit too formal and creates needless extra washing up!

How to serve the meringues
Eat just as they are or:

- Sandwich two together with whipped cream or clotted cream (even better).

- Pop on top of a lemon curd tart for a speedy individual lemon meringue tart.

- Break into smallish pieces and mix with sliced strawberries and whipped or clotted cream in pretty glass dishes for an Eton mess.

- Break into smallish pieces and mix with sliced mixed fruit (such as strawberries, peaches, kiwi fruit and a few raspberries) and whipped or clotted cream in pretty glass dishes for a kind of pavlova sundae.

- Make a snowball ice cream: put a scoop of vanilla ice cream in a bowl, spoon a dollop of whipped or clotted cream over it and arrange a meringue on top at a jaunty angle.

Almond Macaroons

If you can get hold of any rice paper (and it's not easy to find), you can use that to line your baking tray. Once you have allowed the baked macaroons to settle for a while, you can then manoeuvre the whole sheet of rice paper with the macaroons still attached from the baking tray to the cooling rack. Once the macaroons are completely cold, cut each one free and trim the paper neatly with sharp kitchen scissors.

Otherwise, use lightly oiled greaseproof paper to line the tray, leave the macaroons to firm and settle for a while when they first come out of the oven, then peel them away from the greaseproof paper whilst they are still warm. These are beautifully almondy and very traditional looking.

MAKES 9

3 egg whites
½ teaspoon almond extract
150g (5oz) unrefined caster sugar
175g (6oz) ground almonds

Blanched almonds to decorate

You will need a baking tray, lined with lightly oiled greaseproof paper (see above).

1. Preheat the oven to 160°C (fan oven) or equivalent.

2. Separate the eggs and try to avoid including any stringy parts in the white. If any does slip through, remove it between two teaspoons.

3. Add the almond extract to the egg whites and whisk with an electric or hand-held rotary whisk until firm but not too stiff and dry.

Whisk in the sugar gradually. Fold in the ground almonds with a tablespoon. The mixture will become quite stiff.

4. Get yourself a large plate and, using 2 dessertspoons, arrange 9 equal blobs of the mixture on the plate.

5. Wet your hands and pick up each blob carefully, roll it into a ball and put it on the prepared baking tray. The mixture is quite 'loose' but as long as your hands are wet it's an easy (if slightly messy) operation. Make sure the balls are spaced out on the baking tray, to allow for spreading. Put an almond on the top of each one, pressing it in lightly.

6. Bake for about 25 minutes, or until they are golden brown and the tops feel firm. Don't overcook them or they will be too dry inside and you will miss out on the lovely moist chewiness.

7. Don't try to move them as they are very fragile at this stage: leave them to cool and firm up on the tray for a few moments and then peel away from the greaseproof paper.

8. Transfer to a wire rack to finish cooling and once cold, store in an airtight container.

Coconut Macaroons

These are very light, and very lovely.

MAKES 9

3 egg whites
150g (5oz) unrefined caster sugar
175g (6oz) desiccated coconut
Glacé cherries, cut in half, to decorate (optional)

You will need a baking tray, lined with lightly oiled
greaseproof paper.

1. Preheat the oven to 160°C (fan oven) or equivalent.

2. Whisk the egg whites with an electric or hand-held rotary whisk
until firm, but not stiff and dry. Whisk in the sugar gradually. Fold in
the desiccated coconut with a tablespoon. The mixture will become
quite stiff.

3. Get yourself a large plate and, using 2 dessertspoons, arrange
9 equal blobs of the mixture on the plate.

4. Wet your hands and pick up each blob carefully, roll it into a ball
and put it on the prepared baking tray. The mixture is quite 'loose'
but as long as your hands are wet it's an easy (if slightly messy)
operation. Make sure the balls are spaced out on the baking tray, to
allow for spreading. Put half a glacé cherry on the top of each one,
pressing it in lightly.

5. Bake for about 25–30 minutes, or until they are golden brown and
the tops feel firm. As with the previous recipe, don't overcook these.

6. Don't try to move them as they are very fragile at this stage: leave them to cool and firm up on the tray for a few moments and then peel away from the greaseproof paper.

7. Transfer to a wire rack to finish cooling and once cold, store in an airtight container.

Chocolate-drizzled Macaroons

Instead of decorating the **Almond** or **Coconut Macaroons** with an almond or a cherry, try drizzling melted chocolate over them instead.

Break up **50g (2oz) good quality, dark chocolate** and put it into a heatproof bowl. Melt the chocolate in the microwave on high, in 30-second bursts: usually, it will take between 1½ and 2 minutes to melt the chocolate.

Using a spoon, drizzle the chocolate over the now cold macaroons in diagonal lines.

The Three Bears Christmas Cake

If the Three Bears were to make their own Christmas cake, they would probably make a great big, generous cake for Daddy Bear, a nice medium-sized cake for Mummy Bear and a teeny tiny little one for Baby Bear. It's useful to be able to make different-sized Christmas cakes: you can share them around the family and give the smaller ones away as gifts. Options are also given for round-, square- and bar-shaped cakes.

Big, generous cake

This recipe will make one traditional 23cm (9in) round cake, baked in a loose-bottomed tin. If you would prefer to use a square tin for the same amount of mixture you will need a 20cm (8in) one. (The discrepancy in measurement is due to something complicated to do with surface area!)

Medium-sized cake

Alternatively, you can make two medium-sized cakes. There is enough mixture to distribute equally between two 18cm (7in) round, loose-bottomed cake tins or two 450g (1lb) loaf tins. You can use one of each if you prefer: whichever you choose, the two cakes will bake happily side by side.

Miniature cakes

You could also make some dinky round miniature Christmas cakes in a 12-cup muffin tin, or miniature bar cakes in some of those tiny loaf tins you can buy, usually in packs of 6. Since these are quite pricey, you might like to use a combination of the muffin tin and the loaf tins together and make a mixed batch. (You don't actually need cake cases but Christmassy ones can look very festive for the round ones.) The mixture is enough for 30 little cakes, but you may prefer to make 1 medium-sized cake with half the mixture and 15 little cakes with the other half. When filling the medium tin, whether it is round or loaf-shaped, fill the mixture to a depth of 4.5cm (1³/₄in). Bake the medium and small sizes separately as they will need different cooking times, otherwise by the time you have got the smaller ones out of the oven you have lost too much heat.

175g (6oz) raisins
175g (6oz) currants
175g (6oz) sultanas
175g (6oz) butter
225g (8oz) soft dark brown sugar
½ teaspoon each of cinnamon, ground ginger and mixed spice
220ml (7fl oz) water
30ml (1fl oz) brandy
50g (2oz) glacé or dried sour cherries

300g (10oz) fresh self-raising flour
or
300g (10oz) plain flour
2 level teaspoons baking powder

3 very fresh eggs, beaten
50g (2oz) candied peel, finely sliced and cut into small pieces

1. Put the raisins, currants and sultanas, and dried cherries if you are using them, into a large saucepan with the butter, sugar, spices and water. Bring it all to the boil and simmer gently for 5 minutes. Leave to cool.

2. Grease the tin(s) of your choice (line the large and medium ones).

3. Preheat the oven to 150°C (fan oven) or equivalent *for all cake sizes*.

4. Once cold, stir in the brandy and cut the glacé cherries, if you are using them, into quarters and dust in a little of the flour. Sieve the rest of the flour into the mixture with the eggs. Stir in the floured or dried cherries and candied peel. Stir everything together thoroughly.

5. Pour the mixture into the prepared tin(s) and tuck a piece of greaseproof paper loosely round the big and medium cakes. (There is no need to do this with the miniature ones.)

6. Bake the big cake for 1¼ hours until it is firm to the touch and a skewer inserted comes out clean. You may find a square cake will take slightly longer: watch the corners as they can catch and be prepared to turn the cake round if your oven doesn't heat evenly.

7. Bake the medium cakes together, side-by-side in the oven, for about 1¼ hours. Test earlier if your oven is very fierce. The round and the loaf versions will take about the same time to cook.

8. If you are baking one medium cake by itself it will still take about 1¼ hours. Again, test earlier if your oven is very fierce.

9. For the miniature cakes, fill the tins barely half full, as you want them to be fairly flat on top and not too domed. Smooth the top of each little cake gently with a teaspoon and bake for about 20 minutes. You may find the little loaf shapes bake a fraction more quickly. As always, they are ready when firm to the touch and a skewer inserted comes out clean.

10. Leave the cakes to cool in the tin and contract before turning out onto a wire rack to cool completely. The cakes in the miniature loaf tins should come out very easily. There is no need to poke about with a knife, which may scratch the tins: give them a sharp tap on the bottom if they seem reluctant.

11. When cold, wrap the cakes in clean greaseproof paper and store in a tin until ready to ice, just before Christmas. (Try not to bake the tiny ones too early, as they can dry out more quickly.)

✓ Useful notes
• If you are using dried sour cherries rather than glacé cherries, you may also like to try dried cranberries for a change: they are absolutely delicious.

• You may wonder why the large and medium cakes take the same length of time to cook: this is because the tins are filled to a similar depth.

Finally, just to warm you up for all those cracker jokes to come: What is the best thing to put into a Christmas cake? *Teeth.*

A few days before Christmas cover your cake with marzipan and, if you have time, leave it to dry out slightly for a day or two before icing. You will need to cover the cake with apricot or marmalade glaze before you put on the marzipan. You can buy readymade marzipan and roll-on icing but it is really easy to make the marzipan and icing yourself, as follows, and they then become elements of the cake that taste lovely in their own right. You have something you actually want to eat rather than just a bit of decoration.

Apricot or Marmalade Glaze

This helps to stick the almond paste to the cake. Warm **2 tablespoons of apricot jam or marmalade** (you will need to remove any shreds of peel) until it becomes slightly runny. Brush over the top and sides of your cake with a pastry brush if you have one. If not, use a dessertspoon to spoon it over the top of the cake and then use the back of the spoon to smooth it down and over the sides.

Homemade Almond Paste or Marzipan

Almond paste is very simple to make at home and tastes quite different from the bought version: it's fresh and almondy and not at all cloying. You can make this by hand but a food processor makes it easier.

THIS RECIPE IS SUFFICIENT TO COVER A 23CM (9IN) ROUND CAKE OR TWO 18CM (7IN) ROUND CAKES.

110g (4oz) icing sugar
225g (8oz) ground almonds
1 very fresh egg yolk
$^{1}/_{4}$–$^{1}/_{2}$ teaspoon natural almond extract
3 tablespoons lemon juice

1. Sieve the icing sugar into a bowl and stir in the ground almonds. Tip carefully into the bowl of your food processor. Add the egg yolk, almond extract and lemon juice. Whiz for a few seconds and then stop and scrape the mixture from around the sides into the centre and whiz again. Repeat this a few times. The second the mixture congregates together on the side of the bowl, stop whizzing immediately! If you carry on it will become oily and over-processed.

2. Take the mixture out of the processor, gathering up any loose crumbs and put it onto a large board or worktop dusted with icing sugar. Knead it gently for a few seconds and then roll it into a ball, dusting with more icing sugar as necessary. Dust your rolling pin with icing sugar and carefully roll it flat until it is just a fraction bigger in circumference than the whole surface area of your cake including the top and sides.

3. Lift it carefully onto the glazed cake. You might find it easier to lift it by rolling it round your rolling pin and then unrolling it again over the cake. Using both hands, gently and carefully smooth and shape it round the cake and trim the extra from around the bottom of the cake with a knife. Sieve a little more icing sugar over the top and smooth it gently with your rolling pin: if you happen to have a child's rolling pin it will make this bit much easier. Wrap in clean greaseproof paper and keep in a cool dry place for a couple of days before icing.

Christmas Cake Icing

If you aren't very good at fancy icing, don't worry: this is the perfect opportunity to do a bit of 'rough icing' instead. You don't need to do any piping at all, just pile the icing on, rough it up a bit, and pretend the top of the cake is a snow scene! This has several benefits: it's quick and easy, children can have fun helping, and you can use all your favourite decorations.

THIS RECIPE IS SUFFICIENT TO COVER A 23CM (9IN) ROUND CAKE OR TWO 18CM (7IN) ROUND CAKES.

225g (8oz) icing sugar
Approximately 4 tablespoons lemon juice, sieved through a tea strainer

You will need large palette knife or a flexible 30cm (12in) ruler.

1. Sieve the icing sugar into a large bowl. Make a well in the middle and pour in the lemon juice. Using a wooden spoon gradually stir the juice into the icing sugar until it is all mixed in: it takes longer than you think, but keep at it. When it is all mixed in keep stirring until it is smooth and glossy. It should be fairly stiff but still just pourable.

2. Try icing the cake on a large dinner plate, turned upside down. You can leave it there until the icing has set and it is then relatively easy to lift it onto its serving plate, using a couple of fish slices. This saves getting everything too messy.

3. Spoon the icing on top of your cake a little at a time and help it gently over the top and sides with the back of a tablespoon. It helps if the spoon is wet so have a jug of water to hand.

4. Once the cake is covered, smooth the icing gently with the palette knife or flexible ruler. If you do want to make a snow scene, allow the

icing to set slightly and then rough up the surface slightly with the back of a spoon to simulate drifts of snow. If you like, you can make a path across the middle (this may take several attempts) and arrange your decorations on either side of the path. At this stage, it's quite difficult to manoeuvre the cake into a tin, so cover with a large cake dome or cover loosely with foil.

5. The teeny little Christmas cakes look best if you just ice the tops rather than take the marzipan and icing down the sides as well. Use a 10cm (4in) plain round or fluted cutter to cut out the marzipan for the round cakes and a mini loaf tin to cut out the marzipan to the right size for the loaf-shaped ones. Decorate the little cakes with a single birthday cake candle in white or red – this looks lovely whether the cakes are given away individually or arranged on a plate together for Christmas tea. If you made the bar-shaped cake in a 450g (1lb) loaf tin, again, this shape tends to look better with icing on top only.

Simple Simnel Cake

This is a very simple, straightforward version of Simnel Cake that would be perfect for tea on Easter Sunday. You may like to make the cake a couple of weeks before and top it with the marzipan just before Easter. The 11 balls on top of the cake represent each of the disciples, but without Judas. You can make the cake look even lovelier by filling in the space in the middle with fluffy Easter chicks and coloured eggs or fresh spring flowers from the garden.

200g (7oz) raisins
200g (7oz) currants
200g (7oz) sultanas
175g (6oz) butter
250g (8oz) soft dark brown sugar
½ teaspoon each of cinnamon, ground ginger and mixed spice
250ml (8fl oz) water

300g (10oz) self-raising flour
or
300g (10oz) plain flour
2 level teaspoons baking powder

3 very fresh eggs, beaten

Grease and line a 23cm (9in) loose-bottomed cake tin.

1. Preheat the oven to 150°C (fan oven) or equivalent.

2. Put all the raisins, currants and sultanas into a large saucepan with the butter, sugar, spices and water. Bring it all to the boil and simmer gently for 5 minutes. Leave to cool.

3. Sieve the flour into the mixture and add the eggs. Stir everything together thoroughly.

4. Pour the cake mixture into the prepared tin and cover loosely with greaseproof paper, tucking it underneath to secure. Bake for 1¼ hours until it is firm to the touch and a skewer inserted comes out clean.

5. Leave to cool in the tin slightly before turning transferring to a wire rack to cool completely.

Apricot or Marmalade Glaze
Spread this over the top of the cake before you put on the marzipan. Keep back a little to stick on the marzipan balls.

Individual Simnel Cakes and Miniature Cakes

You could also make round miniature **Simnel Cakes** in a 12-cup muffin tin, or miniature bar cakes in mini-loaf tins. You might like to use a combination of the muffin tin and the loaf tins together and make a mixed batch. The mixture is enough for 30 little cakes, but you may prefer to make one medium-sized cake with half the mixture and 15 little cakes with the other half. When filling the medium tin, whether it is round or loaf-shaped, fill the mixture to a depth of 4.5cm (1¾in). Bake the medium and small sizes separately as they will need different cooking times, otherwise by the time you have got the smaller ones out of the oven you have lost too much heat.

For the miniature cakes, fill the tins barely half full, as you want them to be fairly flat on top and not too domed. Smooth the top of each little cake gently with a teaspoon and bake for about 20 minutes. You may find the little loaf shapes bake a fraction more quickly. As always, they are ready when firm to the touch and a skewer inserted comes out clean.

Leave the cakes to cool in the tin and contract before turning out onto a wire rack to cool completely. The miniature loaf tin cakes should come out very easily. There is no need to poke about with a knife, which may scratch the tins: give them a sharp tap on the bottom if they seem reluctant.

Use a 10cm (4in) plain round or fluted cutter to cut out the marzipan for the round cakes and a mini loaf tin to cut out the marzipan to the right size for the loaf-shaped ones. Decorate the little cakes with a single marzipan ball, a single sugar coated mini egg, a single fresh flower, or vary the batch and have a selection of decorations: you might like to use fluffy chicks on some of the cakes.

Baking a half quantity of cake mixture
If you would like to bake a half quantity of the cake mixture, perhaps to make one medium cake, halve all the ingredients and use two eggs.

Plain Scones and Fruit Scones

*MAKES ABOUT 8–9 SCONES. IF YOU WANT TO MAKE
MORE, MAKE SEPARATE BATCHES, RATHER THAN ONE
BIG ONE – IT'S EASIER TO HANDLE.*

*225g (8oz) plain flour
1 level teaspoon bicarbonate of soda
2 level teaspoons cream of tartar
40g (1½oz) softened butter
25g (1oz) unrefined caster sugar
150ml (¼ pint) semi-skimmed milk, warmed slightly*

*For fruit scones
Add 75g (3oz) of raisins or sultanas or a mixture*

1. Preheat the oven to 200°C (fan oven) or equivalent.

2. Sieve the flour, bicarbonate of soda and cream of tartar into a bowl large enough to give you room to manoeuvre. Rub in the softened butter, stir in the sugar (and fruit if using). Mix the milk in gradually; an ordinary dinner knife works well.

3. Knead gently and place on a floured board. Roll out quite thickly with a floured rolling pin to a generous couple of centimetres or three quarters of an inch, and cut out with a 6cm (2½in) cutter, a fluted one looks professional. Re-roll the trimmings and cut out again (these won't be quite as good as the ones you cut out first).

4. Bake on a greased baking sheet for 8–10 minutes until well risen and golden brown on top. Don't overcook them or they will be too hard. Cool on a wire rack. Eat with butter or strawberry jam and clotted cream.

Scone Bunnies

Very young children aren't always keen on scones with cream and jam but they can be partial to a nice **Scone Bunny** with butter and jam. It's worth cutting out some scones using a rabbit cutter if there are a few children in the party. You can use other novelty cutters if you prefer, but make sure the shapes are fairly simple without any complicated thin little legs and twiddly bits, as they won't work with scone dough.

Savoury Scones

Savoury scones are lovely with a cup of tea in the garden in the summer and they are also a welcome winter treat, served warm from the oven.

Herb Scones

These are gorgeously savoury: eat them fresh from the oven with butter and possibly some thin slices of cheese.

MAKES ABOUT 8–9 SCONES

225g (8oz) plain flour
1 level teaspoon bicarbonate of soda
2 level teaspoons cream of tartar
40g (1½oz) softened butter
10g (½oz) unrefined caster sugar
About 1 level tablespoon dried mixed herbs or a heaped one of finely chopped fresh herbs
150ml (¼pt) semi-skimmed milk, warmed slightly

1. Preheat the oven to 200°C (fan oven) or equivalent.

2. Sieve the flour, bicarbonate of soda and cream of tartar into a bowl large enough to give you room to manoeuvre. Rub in the softened butter and stir in the sugar and herbs. Mix the milk in gradually with a dinner knife.

3. Knead gently and place on a floured board. Roll out quite thickly with a floured rolling pin to a depth of about a centimetre or half an inch, and cut out with a 6cm (2½in) fluted, round cutter. Re-roll the trimmings and cut out again.

4. Bake on a greased baking sheet for about 10 minutes until well risen and golden brown on top. Cool on a wire rack.

Cheese Scones

If you would like to increase the strength of cheese flavour in your scones, do this by using the same amount of cheese but choosing a stronger, more vintage variety. If you add extra cheese instead, the texture of the finished scones can be affected and they may well have a slightly greasy feel to them.

MAKES ABOUT 8–10

225g (8oz) plain flour
1 level teaspoon bicarbonate of soda
2 level teaspoons cream of tartar
Generous pinch of mustard powder
40g (1½oz) softened butter
10g (½oz) unrefined caster sugar
75g (3oz) grated well-flavoured Cheddar cheese, mature if possible
150ml (¼pt) semi-skimmed milk, warmed slightly

1. Preheat the oven to 200°C (fan oven) or equivalent.

2. Sieve the flour, bicarbonate of soda, cream of tartar and mustard powder into a bowl large enough to give you room to manoeuvre, and rub in the softened butter. Stir in the sugar and cheese. Mix the milk in gradually: a dinner knife is ideal for this.

3. Knead gently and place on a floured board. Roll out with a floured rolling pin to a depth of a couple of centimetres or three quarters of an inch, and cut out with a 6cm (2½in) fluted, round cutter. Re-roll the trimmings and cut out again.

4. Bake on a greased baking sheet for 8–10 minutes until well risen and golden brown on top. Cool on a wire rack.

Cheese and Herb Scones

These have a lovely extra savoury flavour: just add both cheese and herbs to the scones on page 127.

Freezing
Scones are best when completely fresh but you can freeze them: allow them to cool completely, put in a freezer bag, secure the top and store in the freezer. You can then whip them out of the freezer an hour or two before guests arrive for tea.

Plain Brown Scones

These have the most beautiful nutty flavour and go really well with cheese. They are also very good with butter and honey.

They are made in exactly the same way as the plain scones on page 124 but use **half plain and half wholemeal flour and cut down the sugar to 10g (½oz)**. Make sure you stir and sieve the two flours together thoroughly first so that they are completely blended.

5. Pastries

The very word 'pastries' is enough to make you think of old-fashioned tiered cake stands and silver cake forks. The recipes that follow are for a tempting selection of nostalgic pastry treats.

Jam or Lemon Curd Tarts

Instead of using a standard tart tin for these, bake them in a mini-muffin tin. You then get dinky little deep jam tarts that could come straight from a high class patisserie counter. If you prefer, you can make these with sweet shortcrust: see **Apple Crumble Tarts**.

MAKES ABOUT 16

160g (6oz) plain flour
Pinch of salt
40g (1½oz) butter, cold and cut into small pieces
40g (1½oz) block vegetable shortening, cold and cut into small pieces
2 tablespoons cold water

Plus: jam (raspberry, strawberry, apricot or blackcurrant) or lemon curd

You will need a 6cm (2½in) fluted cutter and a greased 12-cup mini-muffin tin.

1. Preheat the oven to 180°C (fan oven) or equivalent.

2. Sieve the flour and salt carefully into the bowl of your food processor and add the butter and vegetable shortening. Whiz into fine crumbs. Add the water and whiz until the mixture is starting to come together. Turn it out onto a floured board and knead it lightly until it forms a ball.

3. Roll it out gently with a floured rolling pin to a thickness of just less than half a centimetre. Cut out circles with the cutter and put them into the prepared tins.

4. Fill each tart with no more than a slightly rounded teaspoon of jam or lemon curd: they need to be generously filled but not so much that as the jam or lemon curd heats up it boils out of the tarts.

5. Bake the tarts for 12–14 minutes until the pastry is lightly golden. Keep the tart tins level as you take them out of the oven: if you tilt them the practically molten jam or curd can spill out of the tarts at this stage. Remove from the tin with a small palette knife and cool on a wire rack.

Caution: on no account eat the tarts whilst the jam or curd is still liquidy! You will have the roof of your mouth off!

Little Treacle Tarts

MAKES 16

For the filling
4 tablespoons golden syrup
40g (1½oz) soft dark brown sugar
Juice of 1 lemon, sieved
1 teaspoon vanilla extract
Pinch of salt
About 110g (4oz) white or light wholemeal breadcrumbs (no crusts)

For the pastry
160g (6oz) plain flour
40g (1½oz) butter, cold and cut into small pieces
40g (1½oz) block vegetable shortening, cold and cut into small pieces
Pinch of salt
3 tablespoons cold water

You will also need one or two greased 12-cup tart tins and a 6cm (2¹/₂in) cutter, fluted or plain. If you only have one tin you will need to bake a second batch.

1. Preheat the oven to 180°C (fan oven) or equivalent.

Making the filling
2. Warm the golden syrup and brown sugar gently in a fairly roomy saucepan over a moderate heat for a couple of minutes until it is of pouring consistency. This will take a little longer in cool weather as the syrup will be firmer to start with.

3. Remove from the heat and stir in the lemon juice, vanilla and salt. Once the lemon juice is all incorporated, stir in the breadcrumbs, a few at a time, so they are all coated with syrup. Spoon the mixture into the prepared pastry case and smooth into position. Bake for around 30 minutes, until the top is browning very slightly.

Making the pastry
4. Sieve the flour carefully into the bowl of your food processor and add the butter, vegetable shortening and salt. Whiz into fine crumbs. Add the water and whiz again. Once it is starting to form big crumbs and clump together, turn it out onto a lightly floured board and knead it gently into a ball.

5. Roll it gently with a lightly floured rolling pin to a thickness of just less than half a centimetre.

6. Cut out circles of pastry using a 6cm (2½in) fluted cutter and put into the prepared tins, firming them down gently so that the finished tarts will be a good shape rather than just little saucers of pastry. Put a teaspoonful of the treacle mixture into each tart.

7. Bake for about 15 minutes. Remove from the tin with a small palette knife and cool on a wire rack.

Useful note: making the breadcrumbs
Remove the crusts from the bread and tear the bread into pieces. Whiz briefly in the food processor until fine.

Bakewell Tarts

If you are fond of almonds, there is nothing like a Bakewell tart or two and a cup of fairly strong tea at tea time. The crisp pastry and squidgy frangipane matched with the beautiful flavours of almond and raspberry are a terrific combination.

MAKES 15–16

For the pastry
110g (4oz) plain flour
Pinch of salt
50g (2oz) cold butter, cut into small pieces
1 rounded dessertspoon unrefined caster sugar
2 tablespoons cold water

For the Bakewell topping (or frangipane)
75g (3oz) butter, softened
75g (3oz) unrefined caster sugar
40g (1½oz) plain flour
1 egg, beaten
½ teaspoon almond extract
110g (4oz) ground almonds
2 tablespoons milk

Plus: about 3 tablespoons raspberry jam, preferably seedless

You will need one or two greased 12-cup tart tins and a 6cm (2½in) cutter, fluted or plain. If you only have one tin you will need to bake a second part batch.

1. Preheat the oven to 180°C (fan oven) or equivalent.

Making the pastry

2. Sieve the flour and salt carefully into the bowl of your food processor and add the butter. Whiz into fine crumbs and add the sugar. Whiz again briefly. Add the water and whiz until the mixture is starting to come together. Turn it out onto a floured board and knead it lightly until it forms a ball.

3. Roll it out gently with a floured rolling pin to a thickness of just less than half a centimetre.

4. Cut out 12 circles with the cutter. Transfer them to the prepared tart tin and firm them down gently.

Making the Bakewell topping

5. Whiz the butter and sugar together until light and fluffy. Sieve in the flour and add the egg and almond extract. Whiz briefly and add the ground almonds and milk. Whiz again until thoroughly mixed.

Assembling the tarts

6. Spoon a little jam into the base of each tart and top with a teaspoonful of the Bakewell mixture. Smooth it gently with the back of the teaspoon, especially round the edges, so the jam won't bubble through.

7. Bake for about 15–18 minutes or until the Bakewell topping is just tinged golden and risen and the pastry is cooked. Leave to settle for a few moments then ease from the tin with a small palette knife and cool on a wire rack. Eat warm (not hot) or cold.

Almond Tarts

Bake the **Bakewell Tarts** as in the previous recipe but, instead of leaving them plain, scatter flaked almonds over the top of the tarts and press down lightly before they go into the oven. They look beautiful and taste delicious with a nicely contrasting crunch.

Coconut Tarts

These are made in exactly the same way as the **Bakewell Tarts** and **Almond Tarts** but with desiccated coconut for texture and flavour rather than the ground almonds and almond extract.

MAKES 15–16

For the pastry
110g (4oz) plain flour
Pinch of salt
50g (2oz) cold butter, cut into small pieces
1 rounded dessertspoon unrefined caster sugar
2 tablespoons cold water

For the coconut topping
75g (3oz) butter, softened
75g (3oz) sugar
40g (1½oz) plain flour
1 egg, beaten
110g (4oz) desiccated coconut
2 tablespoons milk

Plus: about 3 tablespoons raspberry jam, preferably seedless

You will need one or two greased 12-cup tart tins and a 6cm (2½in) cutter, fluted or plain. If you only have one tin you will need to bake a second part batch.

1. Preheat the oven to 180°C (fan oven) or equivalent.

Making the pastry
2. Sieve the flour and salt carefully into the bowl of your food processor and add the butter. Whiz into fine crumbs and add the sugar. Whiz again briefly. Add the water and whiz until the mixture is starting to come together. Turn it out onto a floured board and knead it lightly until it forms a ball.

3. Roll it out gently with a floured rolling pin to a thickness of just less than half a centimetre.

4. Cut out 12 circles with the cutter. Transfer them to the prepared tart tin and firm them down gently.

Making the coconut topping
5. Whiz the butter and sugar together until light and fluffy. Sieve in the flour and add the egg. Whiz briefly and add the desiccated coconut and milk. Whiz again until thoroughly mixed.

Assembling the tarts
6. Spoon a little jam into the base of each tart and top with a teaspoonful of the coconut mixture. Smooth it gently with the back of the teaspoon, especially round the edges so the jam won't bubble through.

7. Bake for about 15–18 minutes or until the coconut topping is just tinged golden and risen and the pastry is cooked. Leave to settle for a few moments then ease from the tin with a small palette knife and cool on a wire rack. Eat warm (not hot) or cold.

Apple Crumble Tarts

You really only need 12 teaspoons of crumble for this recipe: this
equates to a little less than a quarter of a 225g (8oz) mix. Instructions
have been given for the full amount, as it is very difficult to mix the
very small amount needed successfully. This way, you have enough to
make a crumble for lunchtime and the tarts for tea. Alternatively, you
could freeze all but 12 spoonfuls of crumble for another day. You can
freeze crumble for a short time, but don't leave it in the freezer for
weeks and months as it starts to taste a bit stale and 'airy'.
You could make half the amount of crumble if you prefer, as you
can make 110g (4oz) successfully, and freeze the rest.

MAKES ABOUT 12

For the pastry
110g (4oz) plain flour
Pinch of salt
50g (2oz) cold butter, cut into small pieces
1 rounded dessertspoon unrefined caster sugar
2 tablespoons of cold water

For the crumble (see above for note on quantity)
225g (8oz) plain flour
1 teaspoon baking powder
75g (3oz) butter, softened
75g (3oz) sugar

For the apple filling
Approximately 225g (8oz) eating apples, 3 or 4 Cox's are ideal
1–2 tablespoons apple juice or, failing that, water

You will need a greased 12-cup tart tin
and a 7.5cm (3in) fluted cutter.

1. Preheat the oven to 180°C (fan oven) or equivalent.

Making the pastry
2. Sieve the flour and salt carefully into the bowl of your food processor and add the butter. Whiz into fine crumbs and add the sugar. Whiz again briefly. Add the water and whiz until the mixture is starting to come together. Turn it out onto a floured board and knead it lightly until it forms a ball.

3. Roll it out gently with a floured rolling pin to a thickness of just less than half a centimetre.

4. Cut out 12 circles with the cutter. Transfer them to the prepared tart tin and firm them down gently.

Making the crumble
5. Sieve the flour and baking powder into a roomy bowl and rub in the butter. Stir in the sugar.

Preparing the apples
6. Peel and core the apples. Cut each apple in half and lay face down on your chopping surface. Cut lengthways into half moon slices about a centimetre thick. Cook them gently for a few moments in a splash of apple juice or water until the juices are starting to run and they are softening slightly. Strain off any surplus juice and set aside.

Assembling the tarts
7. Lay the apple slices in the base of each tart so that the base is covered. Top each tart with a spoonful of crumble mixture – don't overdo the crumble as too much crumble can be a bit dry in your mouth!

8. Bake for about 15 minutes or until the crumble is just tinged golden and the pastry is cooked. Ease from the tin with a small palette knife and cool on a wire rack. Eat warm or cold.

Confectioner's Custard or Crème Patisserie

This is a really useful recipe to have in your repertoire and surprisingly easy to make. Keep it covered and it will last for a couple of days in the fridge. Leftover crème patisserie makes a lovely quick pudding with some fruit: soft fruit or peaches are good, and maybe a shortbread biscuit or something similar on the side. Don't add more cornflour than recommended, though, as this is a light confectioner's custard and not a blancmange!

1 egg
1 egg yolk
½ teaspoon vanilla extract
40g (1½oz) unrefined caster sugar
2 level tablespoons cornflour
150ml (¼pt) milk
150ml (¼pt) double cream

A coiled bedspring-type whisk works well for this recipe.

1. Whisk the egg and egg yolk and pass through a sieve. Put the sieved egg into a roomy bowl with the vanilla and sugar and whisk together.

2. Mix the cornflour to a smooth paste with 3–4 tablespoons of cold milk taken from the measured amount.

3. Warm the remaining milk and cream in a smallish heavy-bottomed saucepan until it is almost, but not quite, boiling. Pour it into the cornflour paste, whisking gently all the time. Now whisk the milk and cream and cornflour mixture gently into the eggs, sugar and vanilla.

4. Wash out the saucepan and put the mixture back. Return to the heat and cook gently, stirring constantly, but lightly, with a wooden spoon to start with, and then change to the whisk as the mixture starts to thicken.

5. Once the mixture is thickening, turn off the heat and whisk until smooth and creamy. Don't worry if the mixture seems to turn alarmingly gloopy: keep whisking and it will soon become smooth.

6. Pour into a non-metallic jug or bowl. Allow to cool. A piece of greaseproof paper cut to fit and resting on the surface of the custard will prevent a skin forming. Store covered in the fridge until needed.

Cornflour warning
Cornflour can sometimes act up a bit when you are trying to mix it into a paste. The amount of liquid should be double the amount of cornflour and the liquid should always be cold when mixing with the dry cornflour. If you find yourself with what seems like unmanageable gloop that veers weirdly between wet and dry, even though you have added the correct amount of liquid, pour it through a sieve: it will soon calm down.

Strawberry Tarts

These are the classic elegant tea-time treat.

MAKES 8

For the pastry
160g (6oz) plain flour
Pinch of salt
80g (3oz) cold butter
25g (1oz) unrefined caster sugar
2 tablespoons cold water

Quantity of Crème Patisserie, page 140

To finish
Fresh strawberries

Redcurrant Glaze
4 tablespoons redcurrant jelly
4 tablespoons water

You will need 8 greased, fluted, loose-bottomed, 10cm (4in) tartlet tins, and a baking tray, plus baking beans (preferably ceramic) and greaseproof paper.

1. Preheat the oven to 180°C (fan oven) or equivalent.

2. Cut out 8 circles of greaseproof paper using one of the loose bottoms as a template, and put your baking beans into a jug with a good pouring spout for ease of use.

Making the pastry

3. Sieve the flour and salt carefully into the bowl of your food processor and add the butter. Whiz into fine crumbs and add the sugar. Whiz again briefly. Add the water and whiz until the mixture is starting to come together. Turn it out onto a floured board and knead it lightly until it forms a ball.

4. Divide the pastry into 8 equal pieces. Working with one piece at a time, form it into a ball and roll out gently, keeping it circular, on a very lightly floured board with a lightly floured rolling pin, to a thickness of just less than half a centimetre.

5. Drape the pastry circle over the prepared tin and lower gently into position. Firm the pastry lightly into the fluted sides and coax it into shape. Smooth your hand carefully over the top of the tin so the fluted edges cut through the excess pastry and trim it away, or roll your rolling pin across the top.

6. It is really important that you don't stretch the pastry: if you do it will ping back down the sides of the tins during baking like over-stretched elastic!

7. For ease of use, arrange the tartlet tins on a baking tray. Put a little circle of greaseproof paper in each one and fill almost to the brim with baking beans.

8. Bake for 12–15 minutes or until crisp and golden. Leave to settle and cool in the tin.

9. Once cool, remove the baking beans from the pastry cases. The easiest way is to pick up each pastry case and tip the beans out carefully into an empty washing-up bowl or something similar. Peel away the greaseproof paper circles.

Making the Redcurrant Glaze

10. Melt the redcurrant jelly in a small saucepan with the water, pass through a sieve and allow to cool.

Assembling the finished tarts

11. Spoon enough crème patisserie into each tart to cover the bottom to a depth of about a centimetre to a centimetre or so. Smooth into position with the back of a teaspoon.

12. Slice the strawberries in half and place cut-side down on top of the crème patisserie: try to cover the whole surface of the tart as much as possible.

13. Spoon a small amount of the redcurrant glaze over the top: just enough to give the strawberries a very light coating and carry it to the sides of the tart to cover the crème patisserie.

14. If you own any silver cake forks, now is the time to give them an airing!

Using the pastry trimmings

15. Re-roll the trimmings and use to make some little jam tarts. The re-rolled pastry is fine for small tarts but a little bit over-worked for anything larger.

Fruit Tarts

Make these in exactly the same way as the **Strawberry Tarts** but instead of strawberries, arrange a selection of different fruits on top of the **Crème Patisserie**. Ideal fruits to use are: black or green grapes cut in half and arranged cut-side down, sliced or halved strawberries, sliced kiwi fruit, sliced peaches, raspberries and blueberries.

Instead of using redcurrant jelly, make an **Apricot Glaze** from apricot conserve, in the same way as the **Redcurrant Glaze** in the **Strawberry Tart** recipe.

Eccles Cakes

Currants have a naturally light, citrussy flavour and it's nice to enhance that a bit more with a little finely grated lemon zest, but leave it out if you prefer. Have one of these with a strong cup of tea tucked up in front of the fire on a wintry afternoon, or take one with you 'to keep the cold out' on a bracing winter walk.

MAKES 8

8 dessertspoons currants
25g (1oz) soft brown sugar
25g (1oz) butter
1 tablespoon water
Very finely grated zest of half a lemon
1 sheet of all-butter, ready-rolled, frozen puff pastry, defrosted in the fridge until pliable
1 egg, beaten
Caster sugar to finish

You will need a greased baking tray.

1. Preheat the oven to 200°C (fan oven) or equivalent.

2. Put the currants with the sugar, butter, water and lemon zest into a pan and cook gently until the butter has melted, the sugar has lost its grittiness and the currants are plumping up nicely. Turn off the heat and put a lid on the pan. Leave to cool.

3. Working on an average size of about 230mm x 400mm (9x16in) for your sheet of pastry, put it on a lightly floured board and cut into 8 equal squares with straight, decisive movements, using a sharp, non-serrated knife.

4. Take a square at a time and brush round the edges with beaten egg. Put a dessertspoonful of the currant mixture in the middle.

5. Starting with the corners, draw them into the middle and press them down. Use kitchen scissors to snip away any excess overhang, so the bottom doesn't become too 'wodgy' with too many layers of overlapping pastry that might not cook through properly. Use another dab of beaten egg to stick it down where necessary.

6. You should now have an approximately round shape. Flip it over so the sealed part is underneath, and smooth the sides with the flat of your hands, keeping your hands vertical to the board, and turning the cake round, as you do so. Pat the top gently with your middle three fingers. You should now have a neat round cake.

7. If the pastry has become a little warm during handling, put the shaped cakes in the fridge for 10–15 minutes before the next stage.

8. Add a drop of water to the beaten egg and use it to brush over the cakes. Sprinkle with caster sugar and make several holes with a skewer or the prongs of a carving fork.

9. Lay the cakes on the prepared baking tray and bake for 12–15 minutes or so until they are crisp and golden.

10. There may be a little 'seepage' from the currants on the baking tray when you take them out of the oven, but this is quite normal. Lift them off the tray with a fish slice and transfer to a cooling rack.

11. Eat slightly warm or cold – but not boiling hot as the currants retain the heat for quite a while after they come out of the oven.

12. Once cold, store in an airtight container.

Mince Pies

This recipe is for an all-butter pastry, with a bit more butter and a bit less water than usual. It's easier to make sweet pastry extra nice as the sugar adds to the crumbly texture. If you have made your own mincemeat (see next recipe) then they should be really special.

MAKES 12

180g (6oz) plain flour
Pinch of salt
120g (4oz) cold butter
25g (1oz) unrefined caster sugar
1 tablespoon cold water
12 teaspoons mincemeat (preferably homemade, see next recipe)
A little more caster sugar for finishing

You will need 2 fluted cutters: 7.5cm (3in) and a 6cm (2½in), and a greased 12-cup tart tin.

1. Preheat the oven to 180°C (fan oven) or equivalent.

2. Sieve the flour and salt carefully into the bowl of your food processor and add the butter. Whiz into fine crumbs and add the sugar. Whiz again briefly. Add the water and whiz until the mixture is starting to come together. Turn it out onto a floured board and knead it lightly until it forms a ball.

3. Roll it out gently with a floured rolling pin to a thickness of just less than half a centimetre.

4. Cut out 12 circles with the larger cutter (for the pies) and 12 circles with the smaller cutter (for the lids). As you put the larger circles into the tart tins, firm them down gently so that the finished pies will be a good shape rather than just little saucers of pastry!

5. Put about a teaspoon of mincemeat into each: don't overfill as the mincemeat can boil out. Brush the edge of each lid with water and press them gently onto the pies. If you would like a nice crispy lid, brush each pie with water and sprinkle a little caster sugar over the top. Make a little hole in each lid with the point of a knife.

6. Bake for about 12 minutes or until pale golden. Remove from the tin and cool on a wire rack.

Homemade mincemeat

Homemade mincemeat is far better than anything you can buy readymade. It needs a good two weeks for the flavours to develop properly, so if you are making it for Christmas, aim to make it in good time so it will be ready for your first batches of mince pies.

MAKES APPROXIMATELY 1.5 KG (A LITTLE OVER 3LBS)

225g (8oz) raisins
225g (8oz) sultanas
225g (8oz) currants
225g (8oz) soft dark brown sugar
225g (8oz) firm dessert apple such as Cox's, peeled and
cored (prepared weight)
175g (6oz) shredded suet
110g (4oz) candied peel, cut into fine pieces
Finely grated zest and juice of 1 orange
Finely grated zest and juice of 1 lemon
2–3 teaspoons mixed spice
150ml (¼pt) brandy

1. Put everything into a large bowl, a casserole dish with a lid is ideal. When you add the apples, grate them on to a clean board and make sure you include all their juice. Strain the orange and lemon juice through a sieve and zest the peel into short pieces rather then long strands.

2. Mix everything together thoroughly and leave overnight in a cool place for the flavours to amalgamate.

3. The next day, give everything a stir and spoon the mixture into sterilised jars. Try to avoid leaving any air pockets: keep turning the jars round to check and push the mincemeat down with a dinner knife if you see any.

Sterilising jars
Wash the jars in hot soapy water and rinse thoroughly. Shake off any excess water and stand on a baking tray. Put into the oven for 10 minutes or so at 160°C or equivalent. Alternatively, you can put them through the hottest cycle of your dishwasher if you have one.

6. Biscuits

Vanilla Biscuits

It's very difficult to eat just one of these light, crisp biscuits as they
are very moreish indeed. They have a beautiful flavour – half a
teaspoon of vanilla extract is exactly right, so don't be tempted to
add a bit more 'for luck' or anything!

MAKES APPROXIMATELY 34 BISCUITS

150g (5oz) butter, slightly softened
110g (4oz) unrefined caster sugar
½ teaspoon good quality vanilla extract (not vanilla flavouring)
1 egg, beaten
200g (7oz) plain flour
2 level teaspoons baking powder

You will need a large, greased baking tray
and a plain 6cm (2½in) cutter.

1. Preheat the oven to 180°C (fan oven) or equivalent.

2. Put the butter and sugar in the bowl of your food processor and
whiz until light and fluffy. Add the vanilla to the egg. Sieve about half
the flour and baking powder carefully over the mixture. Add the egg
and vanilla and sieve the rest of the flour on top. Whiz until the
mixture is just starting to come together and then stop and scrape
any mixture down from the sides. Whiz until the mixture starts to
clump together, then stop the machine. You may have to do this in
stages as the mixture is quite dense, removing the lid and scraping
the mixture down from the sides three or four times, particularly at
the beginning.

3. Scoop the mixture out of the machine and knead it lightly together on a floured board. It's quite soft and delicate to work with so keep everything lightly floured and treat it gently. It is easier to manage if you divide it into two pieces and make the biscuits in two batches. Roll the first piece out to a thickness of about half a centimetre. Cut out rounds with the cutter.

4. Transfer to the prepared baking sheet: use a palette knife to help you, as the mixture is quite delicate. Leave space between the biscuits as they spread out a bit during baking.

5. Bake for 5–7 minutes until they are pale golden, but not at all brown.

6. Repeat for the second batch. If you prefer, you can store the dough in the fridge for a few days or freeze it. Defrost frozen dough overnight in the fridge and take dough out of the fridge 20 minutes or so before you need to use it.

7. Leave dough to cool and harden for a couple of minutes, no more, on the tray, and then transfer to a cooling rack, using a palette knife. (If you leave them on the tray for too long they can become stuck fast and you will have to practically chisel them off, breaking them in the process!)

8. The biscuits are very soft when they come out of the oven, but will harden as they cool. Once they are completely cold, store in an airtight tin.

Almond Biscuits

If you like almond you will love these scrumptious biscuits. The ground almonds firm up the mixture slightly and stop it spreading too much during baking, so you can use a fluted cutter which gives a nice professional look. These biscuits are perfect for afternoon tea and are also good to serve with ice cream or a light mousse or fool.

MAKES APPROXIMATELY 34 BISCUITS

150g (5oz) butter, slightly softened
110g (4oz) unrefined caster sugar
½ teaspoon natural almond extract
1 egg, beaten
150g (5oz) plain flour
2 level teaspoons baking powder
50g (2oz) ground almonds

You will need a large, greased baking tray and a fluted 6cm (2½in) cutter.

1. Preheat the oven to 180°C (fan oven) or equivalent.

2. Put the butter and sugar in the bowl of your food processor and whiz until light and fluffy. Add the almond extract to the egg. Sieve about half the flour and baking powder carefully over the mixture. Add the egg and almond extract and sieve the rest of the flour on top. Whiz briefly and add the ground almonds. Whiz until the mixture is just starting to come together and then stop and scrape any mixture down from the sides. Whiz until the mixture starts to clump together, then stop the machine. You may have to do this in stages as the mixture is quite dense, removing the lid and scraping the mixture down from the sides three or four times, particularly at the beginning.

3. Scoop the mixture out of the machine and knead it lightly together on a floured board. It's quite soft and delicate to work with so keep everything lightly floured and treat it gently. It is easier to manage if you divide it into two pieces and make the biscuits in two batches. Roll the first piece out to a thickness of about half a centimetre. Cut out rounds with the cutter.

4. Transfer to the prepared baking sheet: use a palette knife to help you as the mixture is quite delicate.

5. Bake for 5–7 minutes until they are pale golden, but not at all brown.

6. Repeat for the second batch. If you prefer, you can store the dough in the fridge for a few days or freeze it. Defrost frozen dough overnight in the fridge and take dough out of the fridge 20 minutes or so before you need to use it.

7. Leave to cool and harden for a couple of minutes, no more, on the tray, and then transfer to a cooling rack, using a palette knife. (If you leave them on the tray for too long they can become stuck fast and you will have to practically chisel them off, breaking them in the process!)

8. The biscuits are very soft when they come out of the oven, but will harden as they cool. Once they are completely cold, store in an airtight tin.

Coconut Biscuits

If you are fond of coconut, you will love these gorgeous, slightly crumbly, melt-in-the-mouth biscuits. A round, fluted cutter works perfectly well but if you have a similar size square one it looks really effective. You can mix the dough by hand but it's a bit easier in a food processor.

MAKES APPROXIMATELY 34 BISCUITS

150g (5oz) butter, slightly softened
110g (4oz) unrefined caster sugar
150g (5oz) plain flour
1 egg, beaten
2 level teaspoons baking powder
50g (2oz) desiccated coconut

You will need a large, greased baking tray and a fluted 6cm (2½in) cutter.

1. Preheat the oven to 180°C (fan oven) or equivalent.

2. Put the butter and sugar in the bowl of your food processor and whiz until light and fluffy. Sieve about half the flour carefully over the mixture. Add the egg and sieve the rest of the flour and baking powder on top. Whiz briefly and add the coconut. Whiz until the mixture is just starting to come together and then stop machine. (You may have to stop and scrape the mixture down from the sides a couple of times.)

3. Take the mixture out of the machine and gently finish kneading it together on a floured board.

4. Once the dough is ready it is easier to manage if you divide it into two pieces and make the biscuits in two batches. Roll the first piece out to a thickness of about half a centimetre.

5. Cut out the biscuits and transfer to the prepared baking tray: you may find a palette knife is useful to help you move them across.

6. Bake for 5–7 minutes until they are pale golden, but not at all brown.

7. Repeat for the second batch. If you prefer you can store the dough in the fridge for a few days or freeze it. Defrost frozen dough overnight in the fridge and take dough out of the fridge 20 minutes or so before you need to use it.

Easter Biscuits

Traditionally, Easter Biscuits are a fairly large, round biscuit with fluted edges. You may like to keep to tradition or you may prefer to make them a bit smaller. Alternatively, if you are making them with, or for, children, you can use novelty cutters instead: chicks, bunnies and egg shapes are popular for Easter.

MAKES APPROXIMATELY 24 BISCUITS, DEPENDING ON CUTTER SIZE

110g (4oz) butter, softened
75g (3oz) unrefined caster sugar
200g (7oz) plain flour
¼ teaspoon mixed spice, optional
1 whole egg and 1 egg yolk, beaten

You will need a large, greased baking tray.

1. Preheat the oven to 180°C (fan oven) or equivalent.

2. Put the softened butter and sugar in a large bowl and cream together with a wooden spoon until completely mixed together and fluffy.

3. Sieve the flour (and spice, if using) over the mixture and add the egg and egg yolk. Stir together with the wooden spoon until it is fairly well mixed and most of the flour has been absorbed. It will be quite stiff.

4. You will need to get your hands in now to finish the mixing: the warmth from your hands will help bind everything together. Put the mixture onto a floured board and continue to knead the mixture until you have what looks (and feels) like a large ball of marzipan.

5. Roll out with a floured rolling pin to a thickness of a bit more than a pound coin. Cut out with your chosen cutters and transfer to the prepared baking tray.

6. Bake for 7–8 minutes or until very pale golden. Remove fairly swiftly from the baking tray with a small palette knife, and cool on a wire rack. Sprinkle with caster sugar, if liked. Once cooled, they will keep in an airtight tin for several days.

Malted Muesli Biscuits

These scrummy little biscuits are just the thing to keep you going if energy is flagging a little. They are also great for picnics and lunch boxes or to offer with a sociable cup of tea on a free afternoon.

Instructions are given here using the food processor as it's slightly quicker but you can easily make these biscuits by hand.

MAKES ABOUT 22 BISCUITS

110g (4oz) butter, softened
50g (2oz) soft brown sugar
1 level tablespoon barley malt extract
1 tablespoon milk
110g (4oz) wholemeal flour
110g (4oz) unsweetened muesli
(any large nuts should be chopped into smaller pieces)

You will need a greased baking tray.

1. Preheat the oven to 180°C (fan oven) or equivalent.

2. Whiz the butter and sugar together until combined and fluffy and add the malt extract. Whiz again to combine. Add the milk and wholemeal flour and whiz until thoroughly mixed.

3. Remove the blade from the machine and stir in the muesli, making sure it is evenly distributed throughout the mixture.

4. Take teaspoons of the mixture and roll into balls about the size of a walnut. Space these out evenly on the prepared baking tray. Use a fork to flatten each ball into a disc shape (you are not making fork biscuits as such: the biscuits will spread slightly during baking).

5. Bake for 7–8 minutes until they are just starting to go golden brown around the edges.

6. Leave to settle for a moment or two and then transfer to a wire cooling rack, using a small palette knife. They will still be soft at this stage but will firm up as they cool.

7. Once cool, store in an airtight container. Wrap them closely in foil inside the container to keep them extra fresh.

8. You can eat these warm if you like, once the outside has firmed but the middle is still soft. Also, unfortunately, the uncooked dough is very appealing to the adult palate, so if you thought your days of licking mixing bowls were safely behind you, be on your guard!

Malted Ginger Oat Biscuits

There is something very yummy and appealing to the taste about anything malted. Here, a spoonful is added to these little oaty biscuits.

Instructions are given here using the food processor as it's slightly quicker but you can easily make these biscuits by hand

MAKES ABOUT 22 BISCUITS

110g (4oz) butter, softened
50g (2oz) soft brown sugar
1 level tablespoon barley malt extract
110g (4oz) wholemeal flour
Pinch of salt
1–2 teaspoons ground ginger
1 tablespoon milk
110g (4oz) porridge oats

You will need a greased baking tray.

1. Preheat the oven to 180°C (fan oven) or equivalent.

2. Whiz the butter and sugar together until combined and fluffy and add the malt extract. Whiz again to combine. Add the wholemeal flour, salt, ginger and milk and whiz until thoroughly mixed.

3. Remove the blade from the machine and stir in the oats, a few at a time, making sure they are evenly distributed throughout the mixture.

4. Take teaspoons of the mixture and roll into balls about the size of a walnut. Space these out evenly on the prepared baking tray.

5. Use a fork to flatten each ball into a disc shape (you are not making fork biscuits as such: the biscuits will spread slightly during baking). Aim for each disc to measure roughly 4.5cm 1^3/4in) across. You may find it easier if your hands, and the fork, are slightly wet.

6. Bake for 7–8 minutes until they are just starting to go golden brown around the edges.

7. Leave to settle for a moment or two and then transfer to a wire cooling rack, using a small palette knife. They will still be soft at this stage but will firm up as they cool.

8. Once cool, store in an airtight container. Wrap them closely in foil inside the container to keep them extra fresh.

Gingerbread Biscuits

These delicious, spicy biscuits have the most lovely flavour. If you like, you can eat these warm from the oven, or you can wait until they are cooled and crispy. Either way, they are fabulous with a cup of tea!

MAKES APPROXIMATELY 30 BISCUITS

150g (5oz) butter, softened
150g (5oz) soft, dark brown sugar
225g (8oz) plain flour
1 egg, lightly beaten
Pinch of salt
2 teaspoons baking powder
1½ teaspoons each of ground mixed spice, ginger and cinnamon

You will need a large, greased baking tray and a 6cm (2½in) cutter.

1. Preheat the oven to 180°C (fan oven) or equivalent.

2. Whiz the butter and sugar together in the food processor. Sieve half of the flour over the top and add the egg. Then sieve the rest of the flour over the top with the salt, baking powder and spices and whiz until the mixture begins to gather together. (You may need to stop the machine a couple of times and scrape the dough down from the sides of the bowl with a flexible spatula.) Stop the processor, remove the blade and finish gently kneading the dough together on a lightly floured board.

3. Roll out the dough with a lightly floured rolling pin to roughly half a centimetre thick or a fraction more. There is quite a bit of dough so you may want to work in two batches and, unless your oven is enormous, you will probably need to bake in two batches.

4. Cut out the biscuits and transfer to the prepared baking tray: a small palette knife makes the job easier as the dough is quite soft. Bake for about 7 minutes or until pale golden and very, very, slightly brown at the edges. Leave to settle for a few moments then remove from the tray with a small palette knife and cool on a wire rack. Once cold, store in an airtight container.

Variation
You can make a slightly plainer version of this recipe by using 2 tablespoons of milk instead of the egg.

Picnic Biscuits

These scrumptious biscuits are practically a picnic in themselves.
A couple of these, a crisp apple and a flask of something and
you are all set.

MAKES ABOUT 28–30 BISCUITS

150g (5oz) butter, softened
110g (4oz) soft light brown sugar
150g (5oz) plain flour
2 level teaspoons baking powder
1 egg, beaten
50g (2oz) porridge oats
50g (2oz) desiccated coconut
75g (3oz) raisins and dried cranberries, mixed

You will need a large, greased baking tray.

1. Preheat the oven to 180°C (fan oven) or equivalent.

2. Whiz the softened butter and sugar together until soft and fluffy.
Sieve in half of the flour and baking powder over the surface of the
mixture and add the egg. Sieve in the rest of the flour and baking
powder and whiz briefly.

3. Add the oats and coconut and whiz until thoroughly mixed. You may have to stop the machine a couple of times and scrape the mixture down from the sides with a flexible spatula. You may also want to stir the mixture slightly with a dinner knife as it is quite stiff.

4. Remove the blade from the machine and stir in the raisins and cranberries; a dinner knife works better than a spoon for this.

5. Take generous teaspoons of the mixture and roll into balls about the size of a walnut. Space these out evenly on the prepared baking tray. Use a fork to flatten each ball into a disc shape (you are not making fork biscuits as such: the biscuits will spread slightly during baking). It helps if the fork is wet, so have a jug of water handy.

6. You may need to bake the biscuits in two batches. Bake for 7–8 minutes until they are just starting to go golden brown around the edges.

7. Leave to settle for a moment or two and then transfer to a wire cooling rack, using a small palette knife. They will still be soft at this stage but will firm up as they cool.

8. Once cool, store in an airtight container: wrap them closely in foil inside the container to keep them extra fresh. The finished biscuits are more of a cookie than a crisp biscuit in consistency.

Heart-shaped Shortbread Biscuits

These are just the thing to have with tea served in delicate bone china cups. You don't have to use heart-shaped cutters but they do look very appealing. If you have two sizes of heart cutters it's a good idea to use both sizes: then you can cut out more biscuits each time without re-rolling too much, as well as being able to offer a choice of sizes.

MAKES ABOUT 20 BISCUITS, DEPENDING ON CUTTER SIZE

110g (4oz) butter, softened
50g (2oz) unrefined caster sugar – plus a little more
for rolling and sifting
175g (6oz) plain flour

You will need a greased baking tray.

1. Preheat the oven to 140°C (fan oven) or equivalent.

2. Put the softened butter in a bowl and half stir, half beat, with a wooden spoon until it is soft and creamy. Add the sugar and continue until creamed and fluffy.

3. Start adding the flour, a tablespoonful at a time, and beat and stir until it is incorporated. By the time you get to the last couple of spoonfuls of flour it will be a mass of large lumps: finish binding it together with your hands, there is no need to flour them. It will take a couple of minutes to work it all together but the warmth from your hands will help it along.

4. Divide the dough into two batches: it's easier to deal with a smaller amount.

5. Spread the board with a little extra caster sugar, and roll the rolling pin in sugar: there is no need for flour as well.

6. Roll the dough out to the thickness of two pound coins, one on top of each other.

7. Bake for 15–18 minutes or until very pale golden but not at all brown. Leave for a couple of moments then remove fairly swiftly with a small palette knife and cool on a rack.

8. Sprinkle with a little caster sugar whilst still warm.

9. Once cold, store in an airtight container.

Chocolate Biscuit Fridge Cake in a Box

Here is an old favourite: straightforward and yummy. If you prefer, you can make this more traditionally in an 18cm (7in) brownie tin or an 18cm (7in) round, loose-bottomed cake tin.

250g (9oz) digestive biscuits
3 tablespoons golden syrup
75g (3oz) butter, cut into small pieces
110g (4oz) raisins (or sultanas and raisins, mixed)
100g bar milk chocolate

You will need a lightly greased, plastic sandwich box roughly 23 x 18cm (9 x 7in) with a lid.

1. Crush the digestive biscuits: spread them out on a piece of greaseproof paper or a clean tea towel and roll over them a few times with a rolling pin. Take it easy: don't crush them to a fine powder as you want some biscuity texture!

2. Melt the golden syrup gently in a fairly roomy pan and stir in the butter. Keep stirring over a gentle heat until the butter has just melted – this avoids overheating the butter until it is split and oily. Stir the biscuit crumbs, raisins and sultanas into the melted butter and syrup and mix thoroughly.

3. Pile the mixture into the box and smooth it down firmly with the back of a metal spoon – it's easier if the spoon is wet. Make sure the edges are smooth and there isn't a hump in the middle!

4. Break up the chocolate and put it into a heatproof bowl. Melt the chocolate in the microwave on high, in 30-second bursts: usually, it will take between $1^1/2$ and 2 minutes altogether. (Alternatively, melt the chocolate in a bowl over a pan of barely simmering water: choose a bowl that will fit comfortably in the top of the saucepan but without the bottom touching the hot water.)

5. Spread the chocolate carefully over the biscuit mixture: it's a bit of a fiddle but a flexible spatula and a dinner knife will make the job easier.

6. Leave it to cool down for 20 minutes or so and then put the lid on (this avoids a build up of condensation) and chill it in the fridge for a few hours. Once it's starting to chill, you can mark it into squares or slices: use a dinner knife, or a strong plastic picnic knife if you don't want to scratch your box. Loosen the sides and bottom as well.

7. Store in the fridge.

Variations
You can use **dark chocolate** instead of milk chocolate, if you prefer, or half dark, half milk. For extra crunch and goodness, **25g (1oz) chopped blanched almonds** (not flaked) are a nice addition to the biscuit mixture.

7. Tea and Lemonade

Never underestimate the restorative power of a nice hot cup of tea. Much like having a hot bath, most things seem at least a little bit better after a cup of tea. Usually, you might not really think about it, but next time you are feeling a bit ropey and having a cup of tea take the time to notice how you feel – you are almost certain to experience a slight lifting of mood or easing of symptoms!

Tea itself is a fascinating and complex subject. Here is an initial overview of just some of the main tea types written by Daniel Parr, Technical Manager of Clipper Teas.

All tea, whether it's Green, Black, White or Oolong, comes from the same plant, the *Camellia sinensis* in which caffeine naturally occurs. Good quality tea – Green, Black or Oolong – starts out with two leaves and a bud.

Black Tea

For the production of Black Tea the leaves are deliberately put through a fermentation process otherwise known as oxidisation, which causes the green tea leaves to turn dark brown. This helps develop the tannins, flavours and characteristics of Black Tea.

The broad stages of Black Tea manufacture are as follows:

1. Plucking
2. Withering
3. Rolling/Cutting
4. Fermenting (oxidising)
5. Drying
6. Sorting and Grading
7. Packing into bulk containers and packaging

Green Tea

The main difference between the production of Green Tea and Black Tea is that Green Tea does *not* undergo the deliberate fermentation process. Like an apple, when tea leaves are bruised or cut this damages the cells and exposes them to the air, and enzyme activity will naturally turn them brown. Therefore, as opposed to Black Tea, with Green Tea the target is to *stop* as much fermentation from naturally occurring as possible, so that leaves remain as green and fresh as the process allows.

To support this, Green Tea manufacture includes a specific process step that can be referred to as 'fixation'. This effectively involves a short and sudden heat treatment in order to kill or halt enzyme activity.

Depending on the origin and the factory, fixation is generally done by either pan frying, i.e. 'dry heat', or by steaming, i.e. 'wet heat'. The leaves then undergo a further drying stage as do all other teas, to reduce moisture and to act as the final fixation stage prior to grading and sorting.

As with Black Teas, it is a combination of bush varietals, origin, climate, and processing methods and skills that provides such a wide range of styles, flavour profiles and different qualities.

The broad stages of Green Tea manufacture are as follows:

1. Plucking
2. *Withering
3. Steaming/**Pan frying
4. **Rolling/Cutting
5. Drying
6. Sorting and Grading
7. Packing into bulk containers and packaging

*Not all producers will choose to wither green tea
**Steps 3 and 4 are interchangeable in sequence depending on the producer

Green Tea should always be served without milk.

White Tea

White Tea is produced in a very similar manner to Green Tea in that the leaves are not fermented and are intended to stay green. White Tea is said to be one of the least processed teas, which is true when taking into account the number of process steps.

Two important factors that set White Tea apart from Green Tea are the bush varietals used for plucking, and the processing. Bush varietals selected to produce White Tea have a higher level of the small white hairs on the back of the tea leaf, known as 'white hairy down' and this helps to give White Tea its unique character.

White Tea is also *always* withered and has a much longer, or more severe, wither than Green Tea, which also contributes to its unique character and smooth mellow and rounded flavour.

White Tea is traditionally from high grown areas in the Fujian province in South East China, and although other provinces also now commonly produce this tea on a commercial level, Fujian is still one of the main producers.

The broad stages of White Tea manufacture are as follows:

1. Plucking
2. Withering
3. Sorting and Grading
4. Drying
5. Breaking/Cutting*
6. Packing into bulk containers and packaging

*Only if producing tea bag grades

Like Green Tea, White Tea should always be served without milk.

Redbush

Redbush, also known as Rooibos, isn't strictly speaking a tea at all as it is produced from the plant *Aspalathus linearis*, a broom-like member of the legume family of plants that only grows in the Western Cape of South Africa. Unlike normal tea, Redbush is not plucked; instead it is harvested by being cut at approximately half a metre from the ground and the entire cutting is processed, including the leaves, bark and stem.

Like Black Tea, Redbush is deliberately fermented, although by a different method, which helps to develop its reddish-orange colour.

Redbush is an excellent substitute for Black Tea, as it's the non-*camellia sinensis* product that is closest in character to normal Black Tea: both in terms of how the brewed tea is in appearance and colour, as well as how it tastes, although clearly it has its own unique flavour and characteristics.

Redbush has a fresh, clean woody taste and, if it is of a good quality, will have a distinctive caramel-like character.

Like Black Tea, Redbush can be enjoyed equally well with or without milk, yet it has the benefit of being naturally caffeine free.

Darjeeling

An exceptional, light, golden tea with a delicate taste from one of the world's finest growing regions, Darjeeling is regarded as the champagne of teas.

Darjeeling Black Tea is typically light and delicate, with a fresh, vibrant and distinctive muscatel character that is unique to Darjeeling. For the connoisseur, Darjeeling is best enjoyed black due to its light and delicate nature.

Darjeeling is situated in North West India in the foothills of the Himalayan Mountains. On a clear day Mount Everest can be seen in the distance. Darjeeling is a recognised origin by geographical position, and controls are in place to avoid teas from other nearby areas falsely claiming to be Darjeeling. Darjeeling is set at 6,000 feet above sea level and enjoys a cool climate as a result; this enables the tea to grow slowly, which in turn means the leaves have longer to develop the natural chemical make-up that helps contribute to its distinctive flavour.

Most of the tea bushes in Darjeeling are grown from the China-type bush: *Camellia sinensis var. sinensis*. These China-type bushes have smaller leaves and are better suited to colder climates than the *Camellia sinensis var. assamica*-type bushes that are commonly found in other areas such as Assam or Africa. They tend to be used more for CTC production (cut, tear and curl), as they tend to produce teas with a fuller, richer and heavier taste and liquor whereas the China-type bushes tend to deliver lighter, more fragrant and delicate teas.

Darjeeling Black Teas undergo a much lighter and more delicate fermentation process compared with other Black Teas: the leaves are almost semi-oxidised which can often be seen by the mixture of black, golden and light brown leaves with hints of green noticeable in a fine quality Darjeeling.

The growing of Darjeeling is seasonal and the quality and price of the tea produced depends greatly on the time of year. Typically, the season runs between April and October.

Assam

Assam is the world's largest tea-growing region in North East India, lying on either side of the Brahmaputra River. The Brahmaputra valley lies approximately 120 miles east of Darjeeling, and also borders with Bangladesh, Burma and China.

This part of India experiences high precipitation (or rainfall) during the monsoon period: as much as 10 to 12 inches of rain per day. The daytime temperature rises to about 102°F, creating greenhouse-like conditions of extreme humidity and heat. This tropical climate contributes to Assam's unique malty taste, a feature for which this tea is well known. Owing to the climate and geographical location, like Darjeeling, Assam tea production is very seasonal.

Assam produces many varieties and qualities of both orthodox, and CTC (cut, tear and curl) Black Teas, with the finer quality orthodox teas being produced at the beginning of the season from the first and second flush (or first and second tea crops). The largest part of the season's production takes place between July and September.

CTC production, mainly for the tea bag market, can be produced all season with the better quality teas coming from July production. However, for those tea factories that produce both orthodox and CTC, the focus of production at the quality time at the start of the season will be leafy orthodox teas as these will command the highest value.

A typical good quality Assam will be bright, rich, full-bodied and have a distinctive malty character.

Ceylon

Ceylon teas are basically Sri Lankan teas. The teas are still described in the tea industry as 'Ceylon', as this is how they were traditionally termed when the country was known by its former name of Ceylon. Ceylon produces mainly orthodox teas. Some Estates attempted to convert to CTC (cut, tear and curl) teas in the past, however stiff opposition from India and East Africa, particularly Kenya, meant that many of them switched back to orthodox.

Ceylon produces mostly Black Tea and is traditionally considered a Black Tea producing country. Black Tea is what is talked about mostly when the quality of Ceylon tea is described. However, Ceylon is also capable of producing very high quality Green Teas and as Green Tea's popularity grows in different markets, more producers are starting to diversify into Green Tea as well as Black Tea.

Most of Ceylon's tea production takes part in two areas in the South West of the country at between 3,000 and 8,000 feet above sea-level or elevation. Tea production does occur all year, and is less seasonal than, say, Assam. However, the time of year does impact on the quality being produced. Generally, the best quality teas are produced in the periods from the end of February to the middle of March in the western parts, and from the end of June to the end of August in the eastern parts.

Ceylon produces a vast array of different qualities and styles and these are linked to the different tea-growing regions and elevation. There are six main regions in Sri Lanka: Galle, Dimbula, Uva, Nuwara Eliya, Ratnapura and Kandy. Generally the finer, better teas are high-grown and the lesser quality teas are low-grown.

- **Low-grown:** 1,500–1,800 ft above sea level – these are of general good quality, colour and strength but lacking in distinctive and vibrant flavour and character.
- **Mid-grown:** 1,800–3,500 ft above sea level – these are of general better quality than the low-grown, with good colour and rich flavour.
- **High-grown:** 3,500–7,500 ft above sea level – these are the best quality teas with a golden colour and highly refined, intense and distinguished flavour.

In general terms, a good quality black Ceylon tea will deliver a bright golden colour and a brisk, crisp taste with a reminiscence of citrus. Ceylon tea is excellent as a single origin tea or for use in a blend. However, due to the more recent higher cost of production and therefore purchase price, in Sri Lanka versus other big Black Tea producers such as Kenya and Assam less and less Ceylon tea is being used in blends being offered by UK tea brands.

China

Tea was discovered in China, and is believed to have been cultivated since before the birth of Christ. Owing to the long history of tea production in China and the sheer size of the country and distribution of tea production, throughout so many different areas with different cultural backgrounds, China has developed the widest range of teas in the world. They can also be considered some of the finest teas and the most expensive. In fact, there are several thousand different varieties of tea in China so it is impossible to go into any real detail here.

The best tea is grown in the mountains at higher elevations; however, tea is also grown at lower elevations on flatter land as well. Tea is grown in many different provinces, mainly in the South East part of the country: some of which include Fujian, Zhejiang, Hubei, Yunnan and Hunan.

The type of production in China is orthodox although techniques vary dramatically between different producers, depending on the area and on the teas being produced. In fact, many speciality teas are still made by hand, as the delicate nature of the teas can be difficult to replicate using machinery.

In general, China produces the following main tea types: Green, White, Yellow, Oolong, Black, Pu-erh and Lapsang Souchong. Traditionally, and generally, Chinese people do not drink their tea with milk, and therefore have developed the teas in this way. Even the Black Tea China produces was not developed to be drunk with milk, although it may be drunk this way on occasion: if used in Europe to produce an Earl Grey product, for example. However, Chinese Black

Tea would not be suited to an English breakfast-style product, based on its characteristics.

China is one of the only tea-producing countries in the world where the most expensive teas are generally sold into the domestic market and the less expensive teas are exported. This is a direct reflection of how important Chinese people regard tea to be.

Earl Grey

'Earl Grey' is a fancy name or descriptive term for a certain type of tea blend, whereby Black Tea is blended with bergamot oil or flavouring. Depending on the brand, the quality and taste profile of bergamot will differ.

However, in general terms, Bergamot provides a deeply refreshing citrus flavour that can also carry some slight floral notes. The tea used in Earl Grey, whether loose leaf or tea bags, is generally always selected to give a light and delicate liquor and colour, so as to compliment the Bergamot, rather than compete against it.

For this reason, orthodox teas are almost always used rather than CTCs with origins such as China, South India and sometimes Sri Lanka being common.

English Breakfast

'English Breakfast' is a fancy name attributed to a certain type of tea blend based on its quality characteristics, rather than any particular requirements over blend make-up or tea origins.

A good English Breakfast tea will generally be a premium quality Black Tea suited to the typical English market: it will be of good strength, have a rich and full flavour and be bright in colour ideal for drinking with milk.

On this basis, many English Breakfast products will be blends of Assam, Kenya (sometimes other East African countries such as Rwanda or Uganda) and sometimes Sri Lanka.

Bring Back the Teapot!

Although the usual method of making tea these days seems to be to give a tea bag a quick dunk in a mug of hot water, you can't beat making it in a teapot for flavour. It's also a small, calming ritual in what may otherwise be quite a frantic day.

If you frequently make tea for one, it's worth investing in a one-cup teapot. If you try to make a small amount of tea in a larger pot, by the time the tea has brewed it will have lost too much heat and won't be hot enough.

Use a small pot and fill it to the top with water. By the time it has brewed it will be just the right temperature. Bag-in-a-mug tea tends to be scalding hot with a thin and papery flavour, unless you have flattened the bag on the side of the mug with a spoon, in which case it can taste a bit 'stewed'.

Making the perfect cup of tea in a pot takes barely any more time and is less messy, as it doesn't involve trailing the dripping bag across the kitchen balanced on a teaspoon!

Boil the kettle using freshly drawn water.

Take a little water from the kettle before it boils and warm your teapot, swilling the water round and discarding it.

Put in your tea bag(s) or loose leaves.

Take the teapot to the kettle, so that when it boils there is no delay and the water doesn't go off the boil.

Fill the teapot with the boiling water and leave to steep or brew for 3–5 minutes before pouring.

Lie down and relax with two teabags

Squeeze the excess tea from a couple of used teabags and put them in the fridge to chill. Lie down for ten minutes (longer if possible) with a chilled teabag over each eye. It's incredibly soothing and relaxing.

Proper Old-fashioned Lemonade

A summer's day in the garden, bees buzzing, flowers blooming, birds singing, a relaxing chair and an ice-cold glass of lemonade: bliss!

5 large plump fresh lemons (try to buy unwaxed)
110–150g (4–5oz) unrefined granulated sugar
1 litre (1¾pt) cold water
Small amount of boiling water

1. If you suspect the lemons are waxed, wash and scrub them thoroughly in hot soapy water, rinse and pat dry. Peel 4 of the lemons very thinly: a swivel peeler works well. Try to avoid cutting into the white pith as it's very bitter and will taint the finished lemonade.

2. Put the sugar into a saucepan with just enough water to cover and simmer gently until the sugar has completely melted and lost its grittiness. Cool slightly and pour into a heatproof jug. Add the lemon peel and leave to infuse and cool.

3. Once cool, squeeze the juice from the 4 peeled lemons and pour into the jug – don't sieve it yet. Add the water, stir well, cover and chill for a couple of hours.

4. Finally, cut the fifth lemon in half, squeeze half into the jug and slice the other half thinly. Check for sweetness, adding a little more sugar if necessary (use caster sugar at this point as it will dissolve more quickly). Strain into a serving jug and decorate with the lemon slices. You may like to add some ice, but pour the lemonade out quickly if you do: otherwise the ice will melt and the lemonade will be too diluted!

5. Add a few sprigs of fresh lemon balm if you have any in the garden. If you have any lemon verbena, you could add a few of the precious sherbet-lemon tasting leaves.

Lemon and Limeade

This is even zingier than the lemonade and seems more exotic! It is just as thirst quenching and is something a bit different.

3 large plump fresh lemons (try to buy unwaxed)
3 fresh limes
110–150g (4–5oz) unrefined granulated sugar
1 litre (1¾pt) cold water
Small amount boiling water

1. Make the recipe as for Proper Old-fashioned Lemonade, page 181, reserving 1 lemon and 1 lime for the final stage. As before, cut the lemon in half, squeeze half into the jug and slice the other half thinly. Do the same with the lime.

2. Check for sweetness and strain and serve as before.

Index

184